WRITERS AND THEIR WORK

ISOBEL ARMSTRONG
General Editor

BYRON

Silhouette of Byron after his daily ride at Pisa, cut in paper
by Mrs Leigh Hunt. The man-of-the-world Byron.

BYRON

DRUMMOND BONE

© Copyright 2000 by Drummond Bone

First published in 2000 by Northcote House Publishers Ltd, Horndon, Tavistock, Devon, PL19 9NQ, United Kingdom.
Tel: +44 (01822) 810066 Fax: +44 (01822) 810034.

British Library Cataloguing-in-Publication Data
A catalogue record for this book is available from the British Library

ISBN 0-7463-0775-6
Typeset by PDQ Typesetting, Newcastle-under-Lyme
Printed and bound in the United Kingdom

Contents

Preface

This short introduction weaves Byron's life in alternating chapters with studies of his major work to try to suggest the intimate connection between the two, and yet to keep the studies of the work uncluttered by too much contextual information.

It has proved impossible to cover anything like all of Byron's output in such a short space. Even more sadly I have not been able to tackle the letters, journals, and other prose works, which are not only the prime source for our understanding of the poet's life, but are in themselves fascinating works. The letters in particular have great dash and verve, suggesting that the poet of *Don Juan* was there in prose from the early years of the century. They are immensely enjoyable. A selection is available in the Oxford Authors: *Byron* (see 'Note on the Text'), but it is well worth dipping into the thirteen-volume *Byron's Letters and Journals*, edited by Leslie Marchand (John Murray, London, 1973–94).

Acknowledgements

My prime debt is to the lifelong work of Leslie Marchand, who died in 1999. Author of the standard biography of Byron, and editor of the standard edition of his *Letters and Journals*, he was an inspiration to a generation (indeed two or three generations) of Byron scholars. The biographical material in this study, though not necessarily its interpretation, is totally beholden to Marchand's work.

I also owe particular thanks to Isobel Armstrong and Brian Hulme for their patience; to my former students Peter Cochran, Andrew Nicholson and Jane Stabler, for doing their best to keep me up to date; and to the household, on both two legs and four, for putting up with word processor rage.

Biographical Outline

<table>
<tr><td>1788</td><td>George Gordon Byron, born 22 January, London.</td></tr>
<tr><td>1789–98</td><td>Childhood and early education in Aberdeen.</td></tr>
<tr><td>1798</td><td>Inherits title, Lord Byron of Newstead and Rochdale, and moves to Newstead Abbey, Nottinghamshire.</td></tr>
<tr><td>1801–5</td><td>Education at Harrow.</td></tr>
<tr><td>1805–7</td><td>At Cambridge University. Living in Southwell and London when not at Cambridge. At Southwell begins first volume of poems.</td></tr>
<tr><td>1807</td><td>Publication of Hours of Idleness.</td></tr>
<tr><td>1809</td><td>Anonymous publication of English Bards and Scotch Reviewers, a satiric attack on the profession of the critic, following their attacks on Hours of Idleness.</td></tr>
<tr><td>1809–11</td><td>First overseas travels to Portugal, Spain, Malta, Greece, and Turkey. Drafts Childe Harold's Pilgrimage, Cantos I and II.</td></tr>
<tr><td>1812</td><td>10 March, publication of Childe Harold's Pilgrimage, Cantos I and II. Byron finds himself famous overnight.</td></tr>
<tr><td>1812–13</td><td>Lionized by London Society. Many affairs include that with Lady Caroline Lamb and Lady Oxford. Active in politics in the Whig cause. Speaks in the Lords for Catholic emancipation, against the death penalty for frame-breakers, and in support of parliamentary reform.</td></tr>
<tr><td>1813</td><td>Probable affair with his half-sister, Augusta Leigh. Courtship of Annabella Milbanke. Publication of The Giaour, The Bride of Abydos.</td></tr>
<tr><td>1814</td><td>Publication of The Corsair, Lara.</td></tr>
<tr><td>1815</td><td>Marriage to Annabella. Birth of Ada Byron (10 December). Publication of Hebrew Melodies, containing many of Byron's best known lyrics.</td></tr>
</table>

1816   January, separation of Byron and Annabella. On 25 April, Byron leaves England for good. *The Siege of Corinth*, and *Parisina*, the last two Turkish Tales, published.

1816   Spends summer in Switzerland with the Shelleys. Moves in October to Milan and meets Italian revolutionary circle. In November moves on to Venice. From this period date poems such as *The Prisoner of Chillon*, 'Prometheus', 'Darkness', 'The Dream', [Epistle to Augusta], and *Childe Harold* III. *Manfred* is begun.

1817   12 January, birth of Allegra (initially called Alba), daughter of Byron and Claire Clairmont, Mary Shelley's half-sister. Publication of the verse-drama *Manfred*.

1817   Visit to Rome. *Childe Harold* IV written.

1818   Mainly in or near Venice. Publication of *Beppo*. *Don Juan* begun.

1819   Begins affair with the Countess Guiccioli. Her family, the Gambas, deeply involved in revolutionary politics. *Mazeppa* published. Anonymous publication of Cantos I and II of *Don Juan*.

1820   Moves to Ravenna. Teresa Guiccioli separates from her husband.

1821   Byron follows Teresa's exiled family to Pisa. *Marino Faliero* and *The Prophecy of Dante* published. *The Two Foscari, Cain, Sardanapalus* published.

1822   Shelley drowns off Leghorn while returning from a visit to Byron. Allegra dies in a convent.

1822   September, Byron moves with the Gambas to Genoa. *The Vision of Judgment, Werner* published.

1823   July, Byron sails for Greece. He arrives in Cephalonia 3 August. *Heaven and Earth, The Age of Bronze, The Island* published.

1824   Byron arrives on the mainland of Greece, at Missolonghi, 5 January.

1824   19 April. Byron dies in Missolonghi.

Note on the Text

All quotations from Byron's poetry are from *Lord Byron: Complete Poetical Works*, ed. J. J. McGann (Oxford: Clarendon Press, 1980–93). Substantially the same text is available in paperback in *The Oxford Authors: Byron*, ed. J. J. McGann (Oxford, 1986). This single-volume edition includes most of, but not all of, the poems discussed here. It also has a very useful selection of Byron's letters and journals.

All quotations from Byron's letters are from *Byron's Letters and Journals*, ed. Leslie A. Marchand (London: John Murray, 1973–94).

All quotations from Byron's contemporaries are as in Leslie A. Marchand, *Byron: A Biography* (New York: Alfred Knopf, 1957).

Abbreviations

CH   *Child Harold's Pilgrimage*
DJ   *Don Juan*
VJ   *The Vision of Judgment*

1

Aberdeen, Newstead, the Mediterranean

George Gordon Byron was born in London on 22 January 1788, just off Oxford Street, in a house which is now part of Selfridge's Department Store. His mother was Scottish, and as is common Scottish practice, her family name of Gordon was incorporated into his. In fact the poet's parents had sporadically taken the name Gordon, possibly to ensure the Gordon inheritance. His father, John Byron, was from a junior branch of an English aristocratic family, the Byrons of Newstead and Rochdale, and the fifth Baron was the newly born Byron's great uncle. Byron's father was already a widower, with a daughter, Augusta, who was to play a considerable role in the poet's life. Some reports have his first wife driven early to her grave by her husband's profligacy, and profligate he certainly was, though by all accounts also charming and amenable. His own father had also been easy with both women and money, but had also earned as a vice-admiral in the Navy considerable respect for his fearlessness (he was known as 'Foulweather Jack'). Initially Byron's parents had lived in *her* ramshackle castle at Gight near Aberdeen, but pressed by *his* creditors they had decamped to France, from which Mrs Byron returned in order to have her son born in England. The first year of Byron's life was passed on the run from those creditors, but by summer 1789 his mother had settled in Aberdeen. His father seems only to have been present intermittently, finally vanishing to France where he died in 1791.

Byron was then the heir both to a Scottish Calvinist tradition – his mother was not well educated, and a superstitious believer – and to a distinctly cavalier and swashbuckling English heritage. He was also born with a lame right foot, a fact of which the young boy was extremely self-conscious, and which the man never quite forgot. Such a congenital defect was sometimes thought of in superstitious Calvinist circles as a mark of Cain, a signal of damnation. This was a way of thinking which from time to time oppressed the poet, but of which he also made creative use.

Byron's relationship with his mother was stormy, and her tantrums would not have set the poet a model of emotional stability, any more than that he had received from his father's genes. From 7 he was a pupil at Aberdeen Grammar School. By his own record he was an avid reader from well before school days. By his own record too he was introduced early to the adult sexual world by the younger of the two sisters who acted as what we would now call childminders. Whatever the dogmatics of his Aberdeen teachers, it is certain that Byron could not have spent his early childhood without gaining not only the general air of Calvinism which is part of the woof of Scottish culture, but also the considerable knowledge of the Bible which at that time would have gone with it. His first 'love' – an 8-year-old's infatuation for his cousin Mary Duff – stayed with him in memory his whole life, which baffled even himself: 'I certainly had no sexual ideas for years afterwards; and yet my misery, my love for that girl were so violent, that I sometimes doubt if I have ever been really attached since'. His early years could then be thought to have the same mixture of theoretical discipline and actual licence as his genetic mix.

After the death of his father's cousin at the battle of Calvi in Corsica, Byron had been heir to the title, and in May of his eleventh year Byron became the sixth Lord Byron. This was a huge change in the circumstances of his life, not least necessitating a move from Aberdeen to the ancestral home, Newstead Abbey in Nottinghamshire. The Abbey itself, with its ruined Gothic church and two lakes, was scarcely fit to live in, though mother and son did initially make it their home, but 'it was a most romantic spot in which to dream'. When Byron eventually resumed his studies it was first of all in Dulwich, south of London, and then at Harrow.

By this time his peripatetic mother, having let Newstead in order to remain solvent, had settled in Southwell, near Nottingham. Two friendships in particular colour these years.

One was another infatuation, this time with Mary Chaworth, a neighbour at Newstead, an ancestor of whom had been killed in a duel with one of Byron's own ancestors, the so-called 'Wicked Lord'. The other, less written about, but probably more significant friendship, was with a neighbour at Southwell, Elizabeth Pigot. If Mary Chaworth was to receive the honour of being the subject of one of Byron's poems from much later in life (*The Dream*), it was with Elizabeth Pigot that he first had a relationship with a woman as an equal. This was tender but also frank, and verses were exchanged, not only in a spirit of flirtation, but as a civilized pastime. As Byron's relationship with his mother worsened, so his relationship with his half-sister Augusta grew, and she joined Elizabeth in the role of confidante. His relationship with his mother was not helped when the tenant at Newstead, Lord Grey, having apparently made some sexual approach to Byron, proceeded to make up to Mrs Byron, and was not exactly discouraged. By the end of his time at Harrow Byron, who had been an eclectic reader rather than an outstanding student, but had excelled himself at sport, in particular swimming, spent as much of his free time as possible away from his mother, and when he had to be at Southwell, he spent most of his time at the Pigots.

Cambridge University was a bigger stage on which to play, and Byron was following in his father's footsteps, and running up large debts. These were the subject of quarrels not only with his mother and legal advisers, but even with Augusta, from whom he was for a while estranged. It was during his time at Cambridge that the first signs of Byron's bisexuality emerged, but the pattern of all-or-nothing infatuation, this time for a choir-boy, John Edleston, was much the same as before. Elizabeth Pigot maintained her sympathetic watching brief. It was at Cambridge too that Byron began to think of publishing his 'Southwell' verses. These were initially put together in a volume (*Fugitive Pieces*) for the Southwell group and his Cambridge friends, but he was forced to 'water down' the volume following local criticism of its overheated erotic tone. Partly as a result, the volume, which was privately published in January 1807 under the title *Poems on Various Occasions*, was not overly exciting. It was this volume, revised and expanded, which formed the basis of Byron's first true publication, *Hours of*

Idleness, which appeared in June 1807, and was to be the subject of scathing reviews. This experience both further sensitized an already sensitive man, and gave rise to the retaliatory poem *English Bards and Scotch Reviewers*. This is a significant work, not so much in itself as in its revealing Byron's 'turn for satire', and his ease with the manner of Pope and the eighteenth century.

By the time he left Cambridge Byron was in serious debt (to the tune of some £12,000). The traditional 'Grand Tour' of Europe and its cultures, by way of a gentleman's finishing school, was not an option, thanks to the wars which had succeeded one another since the French Revolution. But an overseas trip was both an escape (in the manner of his father), and an answer to what we might now think of as adolescent angst. Byron had by now a wide circle of friends from his university days, but his travelling companion, John Cam Hobhouse, was to remain probably his closest friend for the rest of his life. Hobhouse, later to be the man who coined the term 'Her Majesty's Opposition' for the largest minority party in Parliament, was a very different man from Byron. Although able to drink and jape if necessary, Hobhouse was in many ways a serious soul, always fond of, but not always approving of, his aristocratic friend. Hobhouse's father was an MP, as was Hobhouse himself in later years. But politically Hobhouse was perhaps to prove himself even more radical than Byron, and he was intellectually more astute than Byron would admit (at least to Hobhouse himself). After various false starts, and some notorious parties at Newstead, Byron and Hobhouse left England in July 1809, bound for Lisbon. His travels, which were to take up ten of his fifteen adult years, had begun.

Of all the Romantic poets, Byron travelled by far the most. This is an element in the dissemination of his fame – he quite simply had a personal presence in many countries. His travelling also took him into much closer contact with the daily life of the peoples whose lands he visited than most 'tourists' or students, even those visiting for longer periods but moving in English circles. This gave him an inter-cultural distance from his own Anglo-Scottish upbringing which was not simply a matter of book learning. But it also seems to have produced even from his first trip a sense of rootlessness, which would climax in the exile from England, which lasted from 1816 until his death. Whether or not this had anything to do with his wanderings as an infant, and his move at an early age from a small house in Aberdeen to the scope of an English title, it meant that Byron's sense of alienation, and of the way in which freedom, toleration of others, and isolation interact, was based on physical experience. His experience of the Romantic predicament was physical as well as metaphysical.

Byron and Hobhouse arrived on the Continent at Lisbon, and visited Cintra, which was to remain in the poet's mind, not only as a beauty spot but also as the site of William Beckford's hideaway. Beckford, the author of the Gothic novel *Vathek*, forced to flee England after a homosexual scandal, had lived there in notorious sexual decadence. From Lisbon they made a tour to Seville and Cadiz, and on to Gibraltar and to Malta. The Peninsular War was at its height, and it was while Byron was in Cadiz that news of the British victory at Cuesta reached him. During these months Byron moved in military and diplomatic circles, much closer to the British establishment than in much of his later travels, and there is some evidence to suggest that when he moved further east he gathered information for the military. If so, this would be his first but by no means his last encounter with the shadowy side of politics and military operations. At Malta, en route for Greece, he had an escapade of a different kind, when – to put it simply – an affair nearly led to a duel. This would not be his last brush with this turn of events either.

The travellers disembarked in Patras, on the western edge of the Gulf of Corinth in Greece, on 26 September 1809. Here, on his first day in what he perceived from his classical schooling as the homeland of Western Civilization, Byron noted across the bay the town of Missolonghi, where he was to die fifteen years later.

Byron's first visit to Greece, punctuated by a trip to Turkey proper (Greece was under Turkish rule), saw the writing of *Childe Harold*, Cantos I and II, and not only provided the cultural setting for his early narrative poetry, but also provided him with an experience which set him apart from the mass of his compatriots.

Two events and an issue might help characterize the visit. The first of these is Byron's visits to Ali Pasha and his son Veli, rulers of Albania and the Peloponnesus respectively, nominally under the Sultan, but effectively as absolute rulers. Byron was treated with great courtesy by both, and in return was equally impressed by both. The combination of robber baron and diplomat which characterized both father and son was an obvious prototype of the Byronic hero. Byron also relished the attention, and indeed played up to it, and there is about both encounters a distinctive element of role-playing, not without a sexual undertone. The second event occurred after his visit to Turkey. One day while bathing, Byron saw a party of soldiers carrying a girl in a sack, who was about to be drowned as a punishment for 'illicit love'. Byron apparently knew the girl, though how well he pointedly refused to say, and managed to bribe the soldiers, and, in turn, persuade the authority to commute the sentence of death to one of exile. This episode is characteristic of the 'man of action' in Byron, not at all afraid to become involved in possibly dangerous situations. It also underlines both the exposure to extreme situations, and the liberating effect these had on the poet. In many ways constrained by decorum over petty matters in Britain, he felt free to commit himself in life-and-death issues overseas.

The characteristic issue can be found in Byron's strong views on the transportation of marble statuary, by Lord Elgin, from the Parthenon to Britain. Byron was violently opposed to what he saw as looting. This issue is of course very much alive today. It is however typical of Byron at this period of his life that, unlike the more judicious Hobhouse, he unreservedly took the side of the foreigner with the simple moral case, rather than the British establishment with the more 'sophisticated' position. This 'outsider's' view of political issues remained one of Byron's strong moral cards, though it was to be combined later with a far from naïve view of the 'objectivity' involved.

When Byron finally returned from his travels, he failed to manage to visit his mother before she died, which on top of their poor relations, left him with no small burden of guilt. Other deaths of friends haunted him too. He took up his seat in the House of Lords, and made his first speech against the death penalty for frame-breakers (the 'Luddites' who broke up the machines which took men's work in the textile industry). But his life would change most dramatically on 10 March 1812, when John Murray published *Childe Harold*, Cantos I and II. As Byron himself wrote, 'I awoke one morning and found myself famous'.

2

Childe Harold I and II; the Turkish Tales

What made Byron famous? The topicality of *Childe Harold*, Cantos I and II, the outré character of its hero, and the high ranking identity of its author. The same mix was to keep him famous for the rest of his days as a writer. From time to time the topicality of the work will fade into the background, overwhelmed by the outré characters and a certain literary posturing, but Byron at his best will retain an up-to-the-minute immediacy. Faced with a Europe in chaos, the pilgrim Childe wanders in a vague search for the roots of our civilization, from Portugal on to Spain, following the thread back to its classical Grecian source. The European chaos might herald a rebirth, but the pilgrim is highly sceptical. Greece, in a manner familiar to the eighteenth century, seems to be on the boundary between nature and civilization, a point at which life was both 'all right', and about to go 'all wrong'. But the overriding interest for Byron's readers lay in the 'ennui' of the Childe himself, and in the unorthodox nature of the political opinions shared by Childe and narrator, both of whom the readers instinctively identified with the author.

The literary trick in *Childe Harold* I and II is to make cynical ennui seem both meaningful and admirable. Almost everyone, then and now, has experienced the sense of pointlessness and world-weariness which haunts the Childe. Although a peculiarly adolescent feeling, it is also a highly understandable reaction to a world seemingly out of control (in this case as a result of the Napoleonic wars). But when it is experienced it is anything but meaningful and attractive. To have this feeling projected into a form which inverts its emptiness and presents it as rich and glamorous is powerfully seductive. That this

7

transformation does not actually engage with the causes of the feeling in any very significant way is at least initially neither here nor there. Byron did this in *Childe Harold* in such a way that he set a fashion which has endured in popular fiction to the present day. The 'Byronic Hero', a mixture of dark mystery and glamorous strength, is still the staple of Mills and Boon romantic fiction. It is no surprise that its first incarnation was such an instant success.

Byron claims that he chose the Spenserian stanza in which *Childe Harold* is written because of its flexibility. That it can be flexible as used in *Childe Harold* is true, but not the whole story. It certainly has a broader range than the usual eighteenth-century travelogue, the genre from which *Childe Harold* springs. It is a nine-line stanza, with a couplet at lines 4 and 5, which can either link the two 'halves' of the stanza, or set a barrier between them (with the break hingeing on the couplet rhymes). Lines 8 and 9 also form a couplet, so that the rhyme scheme as a whole is ABABBCBCC. But to think too much of its potential for structural ambiguity makes it sound all too much like Byron's later use of ottava rima, as we shall see later (in chapter 8). It is interesting to note that Byron was however interested even at this early stage of his poetic career in flexibility and the possibilities of quick changes of mood. But the main effect of the stanza is to provide an epic-sounding background against which Byron can mount irony and its near-opposite, melodrama, both as vehicles for the portrait of an *ennuyé* and for bitter political commentary. The very first stanza of the poem lays out its characteristic wares:

> Oh, thou! In Hellas deem'd of heav'nly birth,
> Muse! Form'd or fabled at the minstrel's will!
> Since sham'd full oft by later lyres on earth,
> Mine dares not call thee from the sacred hill:
> Yet there I've wandered by thy vaunted rill;
> Yes! sigh'd o'er Delphi's long-deserted shrine,
> Where, save that feeble fountain, all is still;
> Nor mote my shell awake the weary Nine
> To grace so plain a tale – this lowly lay of mine

(*CH*I.1)

The invocation of the Muse signals the epic or romance-epic context the poem will continue to invoke in the reader. The modern age by comparison with the golden age of Greece is debased. The poet (as will the pilgrim) nevertheless claims privileged knowledge of the source of our civilization. A sceptical note too is introduced – the Muse may only be a fable of the poet, rather than a poetic realization of some goddess. The second stanza shifts us from Greece to England, with carefully chosen ironic archaism:

> Whilome in Albion's isle there dwelt a youth,
> Who ne in virtue's ways did take delight;
> But spent his days in riot most uncouth,
> And vex'd with mirth the drowsy ear of Night.
> Ah, me! in sooth he was a shameless wight,
> Sore given to revel and ungodly glee;
> Few earthly things found favour in his sight
> Save concubines and carnal companie
> And flaunting wassailers of high and low degree
>
> (CHI.2)

The archaism gives the reader a sense of modern conspiratorial distance from the Childe and his epic history, yet also continues to sound the epic bass-line, the *sostenuto* or *leitmotif* as it were of a lost but highly glamorous world of gods and heroes. This note of lost grandeur (which invokes the grandeur as well as the loss) is picked up in the third stanza:

> Childe Harold was he hight: – but whence his name
> And lineage long, it suits me not to say;
> Suffice it, that perchance they were of fame,
> And had been glorious in another day:
> But one sad losel soils a name for aye,
> However mighty in the olden time;
> Nor all that heralds rake from coffin'd clay,
> Nor florid prose, nor honied lies of rhyme
> Can blazon evil deeds, or consecrate a crime.
>
> (CHI.3)

Here, as well as the absent glory, we find two more crucial devices – information hinted at but withheld, and an odd insistence on a single unified explanation of events, which explanation is also withheld. 'One sad losel' has lost the fame of the name, a single crime has cast a curse on the family. But we are not told what, any more than we are told what the family lineage is – 'it suits me not to say'. Byron is creating a sense of meaning and significance, precisely by withholding it. The sense of that-which-is-lost as the only meaningful thing is at the centre of the experience of reading *Childe Harold*, Cantos I and II. It is definable, indeed unitary, single, pure, but it is never defined. Were it to be defined it would be revealed as part of the 'earthly things' which have led to the Childe's (and our) satiety and ennui. In a cynical world, worth can only be protected by being never open to scrutiny. Pure simplicity of moral status can only be 'found' when it can not be found. This literary double-take lies at the heart of the Byronic Hero's narrative. Were his crimes to be defined they would be crimes. But as mysteries they transcend the sordid everyday.

A series of verse narratives in exotic Eastern locations became the 'follow-ups' to the success of *Childe Harold*. These capitalized also on the success of Walter Scott's narrative poems, which they quickly displaced in popular favour. Just like the Childe, the eponymous hero of *Lara* for example has an unknown (if guessable) past. If boredom were emptiness no one would read further, but turned inside out into an emotion positively wallowed in – 'With pleasure drugg'd he almost long'd for woe' – it becomes the mirror in which our own boredom is rendered meaningful. These manoeuvres then underlie not only *Harold* I and II but the sequence of so-called Turkish Tales.

Arguably they are indeed only 'manoeuvres' or literary tricks. By the time one has read the Tales through to *The Siege of Corinth* from 1816 it is easy to be tired of its hero Alp 'Within whose heated bosom throngs/The memory of a thousand wrongs'. The characters are invariably in opposition – they are 'defined' as outsiders, people with 'no' place (except that of having very precisely 'no' place) – the Giaour in his eponymous poem is a Christian in a Muslim world, Alp is a Venetian set against Venice, and so on. They are people who are desperate, either through loss or through obsession with something (usually somebody) unattainable – any suggestion of a 'happy' ending is rigorously avoided since it would render their entire quest merely commonplace. To Walter Scott's recipe they add the gloomy Haroldian outsider (denuded of his and his narrator's irony), but replace Harold's contemporary politics with an Eastern Mediterranean version of Scott's Highland 'frontier'. In a rather facile counterpoint to the fruitless but frenetic action of the heroes and heroines, the poems often stop in freeze-frame, to elevate them above the flow of mundane time, and give a sense of almost painterly or statuesque permanence:

> He wound along – but ere he passed
> One glance he snatched – as if his last –
> A moment checked his wheeling steed –
> A moment breathed him from his speed –
> A moment on his stirrup stood –
> Why looks he o'er the olive wood? –
>
> (Giaour, ll. 216–21)

This moment takes sixteen lines in order not to answer its question. Perhaps more subtle but scarcely less time-consuming – as in another sense it is precisely intended to be – is the opening of *The Corsair*, Canto III, where a suspension of narrative action (for eighteen lines of sunset description) not only creates suspense but lifts the reader out of time:

> Slow sinks, more lovely ere his race be run,
> Along Morea's hills the setting sun;
> Not, as in Northern climes, obscurely bright,
> But one unclouded blaze of living light!
> O'er the hushed deep the yellow beam he throws,
> Gilds the green wave, that trembles as it glows.
> On old Aegina's rock, and Idra's isle,
> The god of gladness sheds his parting smile...
>
> .   .   .   .
>
> Till, darkly shaded from the land and deep,
> Behind his Delphian cliff he sinks to sleep
>
> (Corsair, III.1.1–18)

The following really rather remarkable stanza in *Childe Harold* I (in which every line but the last begins with the definite article) may not be subtle, but it monumentalizes not action but Nature, integrating the elements of a landscape in words in the way a painter might integrate those elements through colour and tone.

> The horrid crags, by toppling convent crown'd,
> The cork-trees hoar that clothe the shaggy steep,
> The mountain-moss by scorching skies imbrown'd,
> The sunken glen, whose sunless shrubs must weep,
> The tender azure of the unruffled deep,

11

> The orange tints that gild the greenest bough,
> The torrents that from cliff to valley leap,
> The vine on high, the willow branch below,
> Mix'd in one mighty scene, with varied beauty glow.
>
> (CHI.19)

Here the key moment is the oxymoron 'one mighty scene, with varied beauty', the composition of 'mere' nature into 'monumental' nature.

These set-pieces were indeed immensely attractive not only to Byron's readers, but to nineteenth-century illustrators. They attempt to escape time by the simplest of literary devices – a narrative suspension. But they do not engage with the problem of time, with the way in which it relativizes the values that we humanly desire to be permanent.

It is worth however having a closer look at a late version of this trope at the opening of *Parisina* (1816), which has some verbal similarities with a very different evening in *Don Juan*:

> It is the hour when from the boughs
> The nightingale's high note is heard;
> It is the hour when lovers' vows
> Seem sweet in every whisper'd word;
> And gentle winds, and waters near,
> Make music to the lonely ear.
> Each flower the dews have lightly wet,
> And in the sky the stars are met,
> And on the wave is deeper blue,
> And on the leaf a browner hue,
> And in the heaven that clear obscure,
> So softly dark, and darkly pure,
> Which follows the decline of day,
> As twilight melts beneath the moon away.
>
> (*Parisina*, ll.1–14)

The stasis of the moment is carried in the repetition 'It is the hour.../It is the hour' and the four consecutive lines beginning with the cumulative 'And'. But other things are at play here too. Fairly obviously the passage introduces an idea of loving encounter – the 'waters near' counteract the isolation of the listener; the dews have touched the flowers; the stars are 'met'; the word 'dark' links two other qualities; the moon 'melts' the twilight. Perhaps less obviously the fixed moment is under gentle siege – the ambiguity of that word 'Seem' is highlighted at the beginning of a line; the twilight 'melting' suggests movement as well as passion; and the intensifying comparatives 'deeper', 'browner', though archetypes of the device which gives a sense of meaning while withholding it (deeper than what? browner than what? – everything and nothing in this world), also suggest movement. This moment 'Which follows the decline of day' (days will always decline) is not quite so stable as it might casually appear to the reader inured to the Turkish Tales 'method'. As a piece of *paysage moralisé* it in fact sets the scene not only for the lovers' meeting but also for their parting. The phrase 'that clear obscure' almost makes explicit the entire paradox (or literary trick) we have been discussing. In this half-light the world appears clear and yet mysterious – too clear and we see by the light of sceptical reason, and yet the mystery cannot be totally baffling or it does not offer the comfort of a sense of meaning. By the time Byron has written this opening to *Parisina* he has written other poems which present the literary trope he has been so fond of as an existential problem – life cannot be manoeuvred by literary sleight of hand.

Other than this exploration of ennui, what else do we find in *Childe Harold* I and II and in the Turkish Tales which helped light the explosion of Byron's celebrity? Related to the up-to-the-minute feel of the poem, and to the outsider-characters of both Childe and his narrator, is the political viewpoint we have described as unorthodox. Those in an inner circle would have known that *Childe Harold* could have been even more unorthodox, had Byron not been persuaded to cancel several inflammatory stanzas, and had some others not been abandoned in draft. But enough were left to make the point unambiguously – the poem is not only critical of the British conduct of the Napoleonic wars, it is critical of the fundamental nature of political power in Europe. British involvement in Spain has not set it free – these lines come at a point where much more vituperation was cut before publication:

> Nor yet, alas! the dreadful work is done,
> Fresh legions pour adown the Pyrenees;
> It deepens still, the work is scarce begun,
> Nor mortal eye the distant end foresees.

(CHI.89.1–4)

The fate of Greece stands as an emblem for the fate of modern Europe:

> Hereditary bondsmen! know ye not
> Who would be free themselves must strike the blow?
>
> .   .   .   .
>
> Greece! Change thy lords, thy state is still the same;
> Thy glorious day is o'er, but not thine years of shame.

(CHII.76.1–2, 8–9)

The recovery of the memories of 'our earliest dreams' – the tales of classical Greece learnt in an eighteenth century childhood – is the goal of the pilgrimage, that boundary line of civilization and nature on which the former is redeemed by the latter. But the recovery is never free from the fact of loss – Greece is part of the slavery of modern Europe:

> And yet how lovely in thine age of woe,
> Land of lost gods and godlike men! art thou!
> Thy vales of ever-green, thy hills of snow
> Proclaim thee Nature's varied favourite now...
>
> Yet are thy skies as blue, thy crags as wild;
> Sweet are thy groves, and verdant are thy fields,
> Thine olive ripe as when Minerva smil'd,
> And still his honied wealth Hymettus yields...
>
> And all the Muse's tales seem truly told,
> Till the sense aches with gazing to behold
> The scenes our earliest dreams have dwelt upon...
>
> The sun, the soil, but not the slave, the same;
> Unchanged in all except its foreign lord

(CHII.85.1–4; 87.1–4; 88.4–6; 89.1–2)

The politics are angry, but they are the politics of the outsider who has no purchase on power – they are the politics of the tourist-observer, angry but without responsibility. The politics of loss in short serve the creation of the texture of the poem rather than informing a political philosophy. Nevertheless, they were sufficiently real to upset the party of government, who (perhaps understandably but certainly exaggeratedly) read the ennobling of ennui as political, rather than critical politics as aiding the ennoblement of ennui.

There have been attempts in criticism (notably in the 1980s) to read the Turkish Tales in strenuously political terms. It is possible, but rarely very enlightening. Allegoric schemes involving Wellington or the Regent have an interest of their own, but represent an extreme reaction – either then in the nineteenth, or now in the twentieth century. On the other hand, what might now to the Western European reader seem the purely personal themes of dislocation and thwarted love are part of a world of violence and quasi-feudal authority which would be very recognizable to the European who had been brought up in the age of the French Revolution, was living through the Napoleonic wars, and to whom the rhetoric of personal freedom and the reality of unlicensed tyranny were the stuff of contemporary life. In our own day, a reader in the Balkans would be much more inclined to take the 'politics' of the Turkish Tales seriously than a reader in the Home Counties of England. But the Turkish Tales are not *Childe Harold* – they are not set in a recognizable present, and though both the Childe's journey and the landscapes of the Tales are exotic for their time – another element in the literary transformation of boredom into glamour (same plot, different scene) – the Tales are exotic to a different degree. To read the Tales politically, one has to read through the spyglass of *Childe Harold*. If topicality, both political and in the more general sense of an immediately recognizable (though at the same time geographically exotic) environment, was one of the elements of *Childe Harold*'s success, it was an element which became obscured by the stress on the existential situation of the central character as the Turkish Tales proceeded.

The truth is that attempts to make the Tales more interesting to the modern reader are just that. Somewhere swirling about in this romantic broth are the sexual and relational politics which are to play a part in the work of Byron's mature years – a sense that power structures are more to do with existing and accidental circumstances than with ideas. But these concerns are to be found much more easily in other poems written in England at the same time as the Turkish Tales, but which have less to do with the fame and form of *Childe Harold*. We will examine these in chapter 4.

3

London: Years of Fame

The years between the publication of *Childe Harold* and Byron's final departure from England in the spring of 1816 were years of private turmoil, public fame, and public notoriety. These were the only years when he was directly involved in British politics, both as a member of the House of Lords and more generally in his identification with the Holland House Whig group. Byron's first speech in the Lords on the frame-breakers' Bill had been very dependent on the party line. His later speech on Catholic emancipation, though passionate, was less well judged from a party point of view, and though his fame was no doubt for a while a useful party asset, it became clear that Byron was not a party animal. His presentation of a petition for parliamentary reform was a positively radical move, but destined to failure. He had little interest in compromises driven by power balances and internecine strife – and, consequently no doubt, little skill. But he did involve himself in the committee work of the House – he was always more practical than his reputation might suggest. Always on the side of the outsider, Byron was by temperament a radical, but equally never an idealist. He could not join the 'radical' establishment, any more than *the* establishment. Despite his identification by the Tory press as one of the political enemy, these years are dominated in reality by his affairs and his disastrous marriage. They are the years of the writing of the Turkish Tales, which were a runaway popular success, but for which he was castigated as a lightweight by his enemies in the press, and of the *Hebrew Melodies*, which contain many of his best known lyric poems.

Byron's sexual affairs, which were bisexual and possibly primarily homosexual during his early travels, were predominantly heterosexual during his years of fame in England.

When under the influence of cultures in which bisexuality was the norm – whether in Cambridge or in Greece – Byron was bisexual; in cultures where it was not, he seems to have been heterosexual. In both, his appetite was clearly strong – from one of his household in Newstead to Lady Oxford, class was never a barrier, either to sex or to affection. His most notorious affair was with Lady Caroline Lamb, but perhaps the strangest aspect of it would have been unknown to the public – namely his correspondence with Lady Melbourne, Caroline's mother-in-law. This correspondence charts Byron's exploits during these years in an extremely frank manner, and in a number of ways provides the best evidence we have of them, certainly from his own point of view. It is also a testimony to his openness to women, at least to those with whom he was not carnally engaged. We remember Elizabeth Pigot from Southwell days, and in the future in Italy lies his relationship with Lady Blessington – though we can surmise that this openness extended to some of his lovers too, and notably to his half-sister Augusta.

The public scandal, of a fairly run-of-the-mill kind, which followed the extravagances of Caroline and the 'mad, bad, and dangerous to know' Lord Byron, was a dress rehearsal for more serious things to come. Although it provided his conservative Tory political enemies with juicy copy, it also contributed to the sales of the Turkish Tales.

Women and the pressures of fame were not the only worry. Money was a constant and not to be underestimated source of harassment. It remained so until the final sale of Newstead after he had left England. There is no doubt that one of Byron's motives in marrying was financial. There were however others, equally suspect. Lady Melbourne has to be blamed for introducing Byron as a likely and suitable suitor for the hand of her niece, Annabella Milbanke, in the full knowledge that one of Byron's reasons for wanting a settled domestic existence was to hide from his love for Augusta. This seems to have begun to develop during the summer of 1813, and to have been reaching danger point by that December. Augusta's own life was none too stable (both she and her husband were hopeless with money), and her instinctive understanding of the poet, after so many years apart, not to mention her sensuality, provided a heady

17

refuge from the pressures of the outside world on a basically highly self-conscious man. Although there is no 'proof', it would seem positively odd in the face of the circumstantial evidence to deny that there was an incestuous affair, and it is likely, though less certain, that Medora Leigh (named as one of Augusta's legitimate family) was the daughter of that affair.

This was not a happy existence into which to marry, and Annabella was almost exactly the wrong kind of person for the mess in which she found herself. She was intelligent, with an interest in mathematics which her daughter would take to considerable heights of achievement. However, she was also naïve (pardonably), and deeply convinced of her own rectitude, crucially lacking in imaginative sympathy. She stayed with the poet for one year and a fortnight, almost exactly. That Byron provoked a break by his verbally violent behaviour, particularly with insinuations about his relationship to Augusta and open flauntings of his other sexual goings-on is more than likely. On the other hand, Annabella's behaviour (again perhaps under-standably particularly since she had just given birth to their daughter Ada) shows signs of obsession even before the separation – after the separation it became almost clinically obsessive. Annabella was convinced that Byron was mad, and indeed *both* showed signs of real irrationality under the various strains they had placed on themselves in the last months of 1815 and the first months of 1816.

When the news of the separation broke, things went from bad to worse. All kinds of rumours were in the air, and most of them probably had some basis in fact. Incest, sodomy, homosexuality. These were not the kind of things which the scandal bearers liked to identify with, unlike the 'mere' adultery with Caroline Lamb. Moreover, the scandal only intensified pressure from his creditors, who (correctly) surmised that the poet might try to escape. At the time and ever since, there has been an intense desire to know 'the reason' for the separation. There is almost certainly no 'single' reason. Byron had shown no real sign of wanting a domestic existence – though he had shown every sign of being unable to cope with the pressures of fame, debt, and the frustrations of a sophisticated and difficult to manage political system. Though he had been involved in theatrical administration at Drury Lane, even that was not a substantial weight in his unbalanced life (and to make matters yet worse it gave him easy access to 'theatrical ladies').

It is easy to overstate how 'different' Byron's psychological position was from 'normal'. Recent biographical speculation has sensationalized Byron's sexuality (for example his interest in Lady Oxford's 11-year-old daughter when he was her mother's lover). There is a tendency either to demonize or appropriate, depending on the biographer's own view of such things. But here was a young person out of university, with no close family other than his half-sister with whom he had not had regular contact in years, thrust into a limelight a considerable part of him felt he did not deserve, besieged by admirers, overwhelmed by debt, and unable to see a career for himself in politics or the artistic establishment. And that does not take into account the family background. A 'nervous breakdown', in modern terms, was understandably on the cards. None of Byron's behaviour is so very unusual, though it may be reprehensible. What has made it interesting is his work.

Here too in Annabella was a young woman, of sheltered upbringing, exposed to a man whose worldly experience was considerable, and whose own considerable imaginative sympathy failed him completely at the very moment when it was most needed. She found herself in an environment so strange as to be genuinely destabilizing and threatening. Of her actions in 1816 it is easy to be understanding. It is less easy, perhaps, from a modern Western perspective to understand her later persecution of Augusta or her (ultimately unsuccessful) attempt to alienate Ada from her father. It is also her reputation's misfortune to be placed between a world-famous husband and a daughter sufficiently talented to have the Pentagon name a computer language in her honour.

Byron's work up until this time is itself obsessed with the paradox that freedom is apparently meaningless. In his years of fame he found out that involvement with a society and with individuals does not necessarily carry meaning with it either. Unable to commit himself, and unable to be free without ennui, Byron might be thought to have reached a philosophical impasse. Whether Byron had reached a position, or whether he was simply in a chaotic mess, Hobhouse led those urging the poet to follow his own instincts and leave England, at least until the mood of the public cooled. And so on 25 April 1816 Byron set sail again, leaving England, as it turned out, for the last time. Hobhouse watched as the ferry set sail: 'the dear fellow pulled off his cap & wav'd it to me – I gazed until I could not distinguish him any longer – God bless him for a gallant spirit and a kind one...'. Two days earlier, only hours after Byron had left his London house, the bailiffs moved in.

4

Explorations: the Lyrics and Short Poems

If it was the real-life journalistic quality of *Childe Harold* that made him famous, and the projection of his hero's personality into the distinctly unreal life of the Turkish Tales that kept him famous, it was to be the inner world of his shorter poems that kept Byron in anthologies and textbooks from Victorian times to the beginning of the 1960s. It is difficult to generalize amidst such a prolific output, but leaving aside the lyrics written before he awoke to find himself famous, it might be reasonable to say that it is the shorter poems, and the poems that draw directly on biographical experience from 1809 to 1816, which first *use* the alienation found in the longer poems. They are the earliest of Byron's output to analyse its dynamics and what might be called its prognosis. It is in this period that we find some of the best known of Byron's lyrics – 'She Walks in Beauty', 'Sun of the Sleepless', 'Stanzas for Music' – some of the most exposed biographical verse – 'When We Two Parted', 'Fare Thee Well', 'Stanzas to [Augusta]', [Epistle to Augusta] – and some of his most famous shorter works – 'Prometheus', 'Darkness', *The Prisoner of Chillon*. This list is as 'Romantic' as the most simple definition of the term could wish, but these poems are rarely simply exploitations of a literary repertoire. Rather they begin to explore that repertoire's underlying logic.

All of the poems in the above list deal with what from an enlightenment or a rationalist point of view are negatives – all seem intent on giving value to that which is 'normally' negative or indeed in wringing value out of that which is searingly negative. In that sense they are similar to the Byronic-Hero poems of chapter 2. But these poems do not deal only in the

21

sleight of hand of literary or 'dramatic' inversion – those techniques examined in chapter 2 which are almost akin to using a photographic negative to obtain a positive print.

'She Walks in Beauty' is best known by its first and most 'Romantic' stanza. Through its three stanzas it modulates from Romantic night to moral day, and from outward beauty and movement to inward purity and repose:

> She walks in beauty, like the night
> Of cloudless climes and starry skies;
> And all that's best of dark and bright
> Meet in her aspect and her eyes:
> Thus mellow'd to that tender light
> Which heaven to gaudy day denies.
>
> One shade the more, one ray the less,
> Had half impair'd the nameless grace
> Which waves in every raven tress,
> Or softly lightens o'er her face;
> Where thoughts serenely sweet express
> How pure, how dear their dwelling place.
>
> And on that cheek, and o'er that brow,
> So soft, so calm, yet eloquent,
> The smiles that win, the tints that glow,
> But tell of days in goodness spent,
> A mind at peace with all below,
> A heart whose love is innocent!

Another way of putting this would be to say that it moves from the unconventional to the conventional, or one might say it moves from the romantic cliché to the moral cliché. Usually the poem is remembered by the former, and the latter is forgotten. But its development is worth noting: stanza 1 at first emphasizes movement and night, modulates to a balance of light and dark, and in the last line re-turns to value night as superior to day. Stanza 2 first emphasizes a rigorous balance (with a repetition of that defining 'one' we have seen before in the *Harold* 'method'), modifies that by nebulousness ('nameless – one of Byron's favourite 'mystery' words) and the reintroduction of movement ('waves in every raven stress'), as in stanza 1 associated with physical beauty, and returns in its last line to stasis. Stanza 3 is organized more simply in a two-part structure rather than a three-part structure, and moves from the physical and from action to the moral beyond action (from 'cheek' and 'smiles' and 'win' and 'glow' to a 'mind at peace' and 'innocent'), the closure of which is gently insisted on by the repetition in the line opening ('A mind/A heart'). Presented schematically, this could be represented ABA, BAB, AB, but the B-element is actually purifying itself as it develops, and might therefore be better represented ABA BAB(i) AB(ii). This is a 'Romantic' poem under deconstruction – the 'necessities' of indefiniteness (escaping the rational and moral light of defining reason and limiting moral code) are superseded by the unambiguous expression of moral certainty. Most readers in the post-Romantic period, which is to say most readers, have instinctively read it in reverse.

'Stanzas for Music' also opens with 'Beauty' in 'romantic' (with a small 'r') fashion.

> There be none of Beauty's daughters
> With a magic like thee;
> And like music on the waters
> Is thy sweet voice to me:
> When, as if its sound were causing
> The charmed ocean's pausing,
> The waves lie still and gleaming,
> And the lulled winds seem dreaming.
>
> And the midnight moon is weaving
> Her bright chain o'er the deep;
> Whose breast is gently heaving,
> As an infant's asleep.
> So the spirit bows before thee,
> To listen and adore thee;
> With a full but soft emotion,
> Like the swell of Summer's ocean.

Another poem of night, this one is wholly soaked in romantic dye, and presents neither a problem transformed, nor a critique of itself. For all its existence as romantic cliché its almost isomorphic nature is actually less a Romantic literary 'device' than the texture of *Harold* or the Tales. That is not to say it is without device. The voice is located in a pause outside of time, in the transforming light of the moon, unselfconscious, innocent, as infinite as the ocean. The temporal 'When' introduces not a moment in time but an expanse outside it. The rhyme is apparently static over five lines and across the two stanzas, as if forward movement is impossible in this suspension of time, though the rhyme's present-participle form suggests unending activity, and the double rhymes differentiate the first two lines of the sequence (cAUsing/pAUsing instead of glEAming/drEAming etc). There *is* action and life, but suspended out of time. The odd (trochaic – dum-de) rhythm of the double rhymes and of the shorter (six-syllable) lines, all but one of which (line 10) require a hesitation before the final two syllables, provide a rhythmic interest, a sense of tension, which builds through the repeated '–ing' rhymes toward the repeated couplet rhyme 'thee/thee'. 'Thee' is the key word in the poem, picking up here at the end its other occurrence (also as rhyme word) in stanza 1. The last couplet returns in its final syllables to the release of energy provided by the unstressed rhymes. The overall effect is a build-up of tension, held in check by the weak rhymes, until the rhythmically regular and repeated strong rhymes of the 'thee' couplet, dying off as the tension is released in the last couplet. It is pretty clearly sexual.

Turning from this quintessential romantic anthology piece to another of Byron's best known lyrics, 'Sun of the Sleepless', we return to Romanticism as an existential problem rather than a state of plenitude. One of the poems written for the musical volume *Hebrew Melodies*, a volume in which there is considerable evidence to show Byron collaborated with the Jewish composer Isaac Nathan rather than simply delivering to him a bundle of poems, 'Sun of the Sleepless' has a revealing earlier existence as part of a longer fragment. As it stands in the collection, it is a lyric of romantic loss, in which the moon is an agent of nostalgia, and memory at once an escape and a horror. The negative light of the moon reveals not what is present, but what is absent. Instead of warming, it chills.

> Sun of the sleepless! melancholy star!
> Whose tearful beam glows tremulously far,
> That show'st the darkness thou canst not dispel,
> How like art thou to joy remembered well!
> So gleams the past, the light of other days,
> Which shines, but warms not with its powerless rays;
> A night-beam Sorrow watcheth to behold,
> Distinct, but distant – clear – but, oh how cold!

The last line is a masterpiece in which the centre is hollowed out, the circular structure of the line enveloping an empty centre. Thus the consonants 'd', and their related non-voiced dentals 't' (which 'close' the sound they make), together with the mid-vowels represented by 'i-s', 'i-n', 'i-s', 'a-n', dominate the first five syllables. The line then breaks awkwardly with a monosyllable – 'clear' – separated from what comes before and after by dashes (the syntax is appositional), and unrelated sonically to anything else so far in the line. The second half of the line begins dominated by open vowels and unclosed syllables, until 'cold' picks up the 'c' of 'clear' (though the vowel sound of 'clear' remains isolated), and dramatically returns the line to a full-close on the sharp 'd' with which it started. The rhythmic and sonic vagueness in the middle of the line mirrors the emptiness of the moon's light, while the renewed symmetry at its close inscribes its death-like precision. The poem flirts with the glamour of loss and its romantic nightscape, but in the end what we are given is loss, and not loss recuperated. This is something different. If we go under the text in the *Hebrew Melodies* collection, the motivating force of the poem becomes clear. The earlier fragment 'continues', as it were:

> Oh, as full thought comes rushing o'er the mind,
> Of all we saw before – to leave behind –
> Of all – but words – what are they? can they give
> A trace of breath to thoughts while yet they live?
> No – ...
>
> .   .   .   .
>
> The strife once o'er, then words may find their way,
> But how enfeebled from the forced delay.
>
> .   .   .   .
>
> Safe on the shore the Artist first must stand –
> And then the pencil trembles in his hand.

> (*Harmodia*, ll. 19–23, 29–30, 33–4)

What is past is not just the memory of things past, not even just the general sense of *temps perdu*, but very specifically the loss, when we express something, of the reality expressed. The light of the moon becomes the light on life shone by the writer – clearer than life perhaps, but always less than life. Behind the nostalgia, there lurks the barrier of consciousness – life made understandable to the mind is life lost. Here in 1814 Byron as a writer is confronting the problem which instinctively he worked around, or worked with, in his presentation of the pilgrim and his 'Turkish' relatives. The business of writing is itself bound up with alienation – the writer is an outsider in a very particular way. Meaning in this view of things is separated from the real. At the centre of the beam of light thrown by the work of the poet there is an emptiness. For the next few years in the shorter poems this emptiness becomes a palpable presence in Byron's work, rather than a subject to be transformed into the best-seller material of the Tales.

The most extreme case is 'Darkness', from 1816. It has antecedents in Coleridge (and a possible occasion in the terrible weather of the summer of 1816!):

> ... The world was void,
> The populous and the powerful – was a lump,
> Seasonless, herbless, treeless, manless, lifeless –
> A lump of death – a chaos of hard clay.
> The rivers, lakes, and ocean all stood still,
> And nothing stirred within their silent depths;
> Ships sailorless lay rotting on the sea,
> And their masts fell down piecemeal; as they dropp'd
> They slept on the abyss without a surge –
> The waves were dead; the tides were in their grave,
> The moon their mistress had expired before;
> The winds were withered in the stagnant air,
> And the clouds perish'd; Darkness had no need
> Of aid from them – She was the universe

('Darkness', ll. 69–82)

This nihilistic vision makes no attempt to convert itself into something it is not. This negative will not print positive. Here there is not even the poet's moon. It is, one might be forgiven by Byron's life at the time for thinking, a place from which one can only come up or go under. This is a cynicism from which even cynical energy has drained. The string of words whose meaning is withdrawn by their suffix ('Seasonless', 'herbless', 'treeless', 'manless', 'lifeless'), the inventionless repetition of 'a lump', the appositional syntax, all have no forward energy, no movement. Time has stopped, and not been stopped by the poem. We as readers do not escape time, we are trapped by its cessation. The last two men alive do not even recognize their enmity in the death-shock of their mutual appearance. Here is Romantic night and darkness taken literally, without literary transformation. The effect is indeed shocking, in an almost obscene way.

The mirror image of 'Darkness' can be found in 'Prometheus', also from that strange and eventful summer of 1816. Here a negative view of existence is wilfully wrenched into a positive. The resistance of Prometheus is the prototype of man's resistance to the indignities of life and the annihilation of death. The poem owes something to Gray's *The Bard*, but the quality of resistance offered is Romantic rather than classical, active rather than passive. In this it is to be contrasted with Shelley's *Prometheus Unbound*, written by Byron's friend in the context not only of this poem but also of the related drama *Manfred* (see page 36). But the Romantic stance of Prometheus is not the same as the literary Romanticism of *Childe Harold*. This is not an indulgence of suffering, but a call to live positively nevertheless. Part of the force of the poem is certainly gained from the classical intertextuality (the invocation of the Prometheus myth), and it could be argued that this is literary sleight of hand, since the point of the poem is the rejection of claims to authority. But the latter part of the poem self-consciously uses the myth as a symbol, and thus distances itself from taking it as a given absolute (as something 'real'). It is an example in a human context, not a poetical–divine revelation. Indeed from stanza 2 to stanza 3 the poem shifts from epic to human in scale or, to put it another way, it shifts from myth to tragedy.

> All that the Thunderer wrung from thee
> Was but the menace which flung back
> On him the torments of thy rack;
> The fate thou didst so well foresee
> But would not to appease him tell;
> And in thy Silence was his Sentence,
> And in his Soul a vain repentance,
> And evil dread so ill dissembled
> That in his hand the lightnings trembled.
>
> Thy Godlike crime was to be kind,
> To render with thy precepts less
> The sum of human wretchedness,
> And strengthen Man with his own mind;
> But baffled as thou wert from high,
> Still in thy patient energy,

In the endurance, and repulse
Of thine impenetrable Spirit,
Which Earth and Heaven could not convulse,
A mighty lesson we inherit:
Thou art a symbol and a sign
To Mortals of their fate and force;
Like thee, Man is in part divine,
A troubled stream from a pure source;
And Man in portions can foresee
His own funereal destiny;
His wretchedness, and his resistance,
And his sad unallied existence:
To which his Spirit may oppose
Itself – an equal to all woes,
And a firm will, and a deep sense,
Which even in torture can descry
Its own concentered recompense,
Triumphant where it dares defy,
And making Death a Victory.

('Prometheus', ll. 26–59)

In this last stanza we find too a very clear statement of a Byronic theme – 'Man is in part divine,/A troubled stream from a pure source' – and one of the first examples of a Byronic solution to this paradox – '[man's] own concentered recompense'. The theme of the admixture in man of a mind encompassing eternity and of a mortal body runs throughout Byron's work. As he moves toward his mature work it increasingly becomes clear that there is no resolution to this tension. However, man can overcome the tension's consequent nihilism by creating his own 'recompense', his own meaning for existence within the confines of existence itself. No resolution can be brought from elsewhere, from the beyond, from divine intervention – such longed for resolutions are illusions or escapism at best, and enslavement at worst. Man must remain 'concentered', within his own boundaries. Only there, paradoxically, lies freedom.

Byron's developing notion of freedom as an inner state might at this period be thought to resemble Shelley's, and to be at moments uncomfortably solipsistic. That is, it can seem to represent a retreat into the self, rather than a transformation of the relationship between self and world. This is arguably the case in the famous 'Sonnet on Chillon' which precedes *The*

Prisoner of Chillon. Byron used the word 'metaphysical' to describe his drama *Manfred*, begun in 1816, but it could be used to describe a general tendency of his work in this period. However a sense of the realities of the outside world is never wholly absent. Although the "Sonnet" begins with a ringing affirmation of freedom as a mental state, the essence of which can only be revealed when the physical body is imprisoned, the poem actually goes on to make the very practical point that imprisoning opponents often has the reverse of the desired effect, and in creating martyrs creates a cause.

> Eternal spirit of the chainless mind!
> Brightest in dungeons, Liberty! thou art,
> For there thy habitation is the heart –
> The heart which love of thee alone can bind;
> And when thy sons to fetters are consigned –
> To fetters, and the damp vault's dayless gloom,
> Their country conquers with their martyrdom,
> And Freedom's fame finds wings on every wind.
>
> Chillon! thy prison is a holy place,
> And thy sad floor an altar – for 'twas trod,
> Until his very steps have left a trace
> Worn, as if thy cold pavement were a sod,
> By Bonnivard! – May none those marks efface!
> For they appeal from tyranny to God.

It is true that it returns at its end to a divine rather than a mundane vision of freedom, and that the opening 'Eternal' is echoed by the closing 'God', but the sestet also introduces the historical case of Bonnivard, and so grounds in reality the 'Fable' of *The Prisoner of Chillon* which follows it. As we shall see later, this inability to allow himself to leave behind the realities of life and the facts of history, either for absorption into some larger benign element or for a 'concentration' within a self which is wholly free of the outside world, was to become a determining characteristic of Byron's major mature work. It is of course related to that simple journalistic interest in the contemporary world evident from *Childe Harold* onwards. Though under stress from the metaphysics of this middle period, this interest never entirely vanishes.

The Prisoner of Chillon itself places as much value on community as it does on inner resourcefulness. Three brothers are imprisoned in Chillon, but the central character is saved from the wasting death that befalls his brothers by empathy with a bird that visits his prison window:

> And it was come to love me when
> None lived to love me so again...

(Prisoner of Chillon, ll. 275–6)

This in turn flows into a new sympathy for his guards, and then into a passage even more reminiscent of Coleridge's *Ancient Mariner* than is the rest of the poem, in which the prisoner sees into the life of the fish swimming by the castle wall. When the guards come to free him, there is a moment when it seems that freedom is a uniquely private matter, a sort of mixture of Haroldian indulgence mixed with the defiance of the Sonnet:

> I learn'd to love despair.
> And thus when they appear'd at last,
> And all my bonds aside were cast,
> These heavy walls to me had grown
> A hermitage – and all my own!

(Prisoner of Chillon, ll. 374–8)

But this is quickly turned again into a matter of relationship and community:

> With spiders I had friendship made,
> And watch'd them in their sullen trade,
> Had seen the mice by moonlight play,
> And why should I feel less than they?
> We were all inmates of one place,
> And I, the monarch of each race,
> Had power to kill – yet, strange to tell!
> In quiet we had learn'd to dwell,
> Nor slew I of my subjects one,
> What Sovereign hath so little done?
> My very chains and I grew friends,
> So much a long communion tends
> To make us what we are: even I
> Regain'd my freedom with a sigh.

(Prisoner of Chillon, ll. 381–94)

The last line above – the last line of the poem – is not only psychologically accurate, but has also a possible philosophical implication – that freedom is not of such great value as community. It would not do to make too much of this, but it

30

does serve to underline that Byron's idea of freedom cannot be totally assimilated to high Romantic solipsism. On the other hand, the ending might be thought to have something too much of the self-pity of a Harold, a reading which in turn has to be weighed against its psychological truth. This uneasiness might best be laid at the door of the kind of community which is actually imaged in *Chillon*. Through Shelley's direct influence, Byron was in 1816 wrestling with a mystical view of nature which drew heavily on Wordsworth and, in this poem particularly, Coleridge. Although in *Chillon* the link with nature is as much a metaphor for human community (see the closing lines above) as it is a type of divine relationship ('Sweet bird ... A visitant from Paradise'), it is not entirely free of this mystical possibility. This does rather soften the poem's political colouring into a more metaphysical hue.

Even the biographical poems of the period are not uniformly direct in their engagement with life. The 'Stanzas to [Augusta]' follow a Romantic literary pattern which is either easily moving or overly obvious depending on taste:

> Though the day of my destiny's over,
> And the star of my fate hath declined,
> Thy soft heart refused to discover
> The faults which so many could find;
> Though thy soul with my grief was acquainted,
> It shrunk not to share it with me,
> And the love which my spirit hath painted
> It never hath found but in *thee*.
>
> From the wreck of the past, which hath perish'd,
> Thus much I at least may recall,
> It hath taught me that what I most cherish'd
> Deserved to be dearest of all:
> In the desert a fountain is springing,
> In the wide waste there still is a tree,
> And a bird in the solitude singing,
> Which speaks to my spirit of *thee*.

(stanzas 1 and 6)

The first and last stanzas quoted above display the tidy art of the poem. Its Romantic–Christian figures (the desert, the fountain, the tree, the bird), are carried by a clever rhythm and rhyme scheme. Triplet openings to the lines move into alternating iambs

31

and trochees at their endings, which, with their associated strong and weak rhymes, produce an interweaving pattern of positive love and negative despair. It is, however, all rather too pat.

The unpublished '[Epistle to Augusta]' is another thing altogether. It is written in the Italian verse form – ottava rima – which Byron was later to adopt for what are now regarded as his most significant works. This stanza consists of eight lines of decasyllables rhyming ABABABCC. The thrice-repeated rhymes make it difficult in English, and tend to throw into relief both these rhymes and the contrast of the concluding couplet. Although here he uses virtually none of the self-conscious devices of the later poems in the same form, there is the same conversational tone, and it is oddly resonant that one of his most personal of poems prefigures his mature 'voice', even if almost accidentally. It is a tense struggle in a mire of loneliness, defiance, a desire to reconnect himself to the world around, a sense of freedom, and a not-quite-won struggle for resignation. Byronic tropes litter the poem – the Promethean desire to leave the mortal 'clay' behind and the temptation of suicide to be found in *Manfred*; the sense of the freedom in exile captured in the reference to the penultimate line of *Paradise Lost* 'The world is all before me' (a reference also found in *Childe Harold*); individual life and the life of empires together likened to vanishing sea-spray, to be found later again in *Don Juan* XV; and most importantly the constant shying away from the consolations of nature and a return to the overpowering sense of isolation, which in turn might, but might not, be the ground of freedom:

> Mine were my faults – and mine be their reward –
> My whole life was a contest – since the day
> That gave me being gave me that which marred
> The gift – a fate or will that walked astray –
> And I at times have found the struggle hard
> And thought of shaking off my bonds of clay –
> But now I fain would for a time survive
> If but to see what next can well arrive.
>
> Here are the Alpine landscapes – which create
> A fund for contemplation – to admire
> Is a brief feeling of a trivial date –
> But something worthier do such scenes inspire:
> Here to be lonely is not desolate –

For much I view which I could most desire –
And above all a lake I can behold –
Lovelier – not dearer – than our own of old.

Oh that thou wert but with me! – but I grow
The fool of my own wishes – and forget
The solitude which I have vaunted so
Has lost its praise in this but one regret –
There may be others which I less may show –
I am not of the plaintive mood – and yet
I feel an ebb in my philosophy
And the tide rising in my altered eye.

([Epistle to Augusta], sts 4, 8–9)

In the first of the stanzas quoted above, no reader should miss the play on the words 'that walked astray', which refer not only to a metaphoric individualism but to the fact that at his birth Byron was born lame – in his case being born was literally a deformity. The question of personal responsibility which saturates this stanza is the central concern of the great drama *Manfred* – freedom bears this burden of responsibility if it is to be truly free. There are even verbal echoes of Manfred's final long speech – both poems date from the summer of 1816. But in the shoulder-shrug of the concluding couplet lies a notable hint of the tone of acceptance found in the ottava rima poems which lie beyond *Manfred*. The second pair of stanzas moves from an attempt to be absorbed in nature, not to the stoically borne responsibilities of individual freedom, but to an honest self-pity springing from loneliness. The poem's conclusion aspires to affirmation of the at least life-long, if not permanent, value of love. But the syntax is so fragmented that there is little sense of resolution – it almost seems a struggle to speak the words:

For thee – my own sweet Sister – in thy heart
I know myself secure – as thou in mine
We were and are – I am – even as thou art –
Beings – who ne'er each other can resign
It is the same together or apart –
From life's commencement to its slow decline –
We are entwined – let death come slow or fast
The tie which bound the first endures the last.

([Epistle to Augusta] st. 16)

At the end of chapter 2, I compared the Turkish Tales to a kind

33

of unrefined broth in which Byron's insistence on the world before him could squidgily be discerned. In a much more subtle way, the agonizingly personal [Epistle to Augusta] contains in a tissue of autobiography the problems and, possibly, the solutions, which Byron's public work would wrestle with, and overcome, in the years from 1816 until his death. It is still difficult to see how either the darkly literary Romanticism, or the tense doubt of both world and self, in the early years of exile, could transform themselves into the almost Shakespearean comedy of his *Don Juan* style, yet that transformation was to take less than two years.

5

First Year of Exile: Switzerland

Byron's journey (with Venice as its proclaimed destination) took him to the field of the battle of Waterloo, and on down the Rhine to Switzerland. This was to be the trajectory of *Childe Harold* III. He spent the notoriously wet summer of 1816 in Switzerland, based at Cologny on Lake Geneva, in a house known as the Villa Diodati. He also spent some weeks touring in the Bernese Alps. Intensely influenced by his surroundings, it was over this period that he wrote most of the first draft of *Manfred*, as well as a number of significant shorter poems, including *Prometheus* and *The Prisoner of Chillon*. He did not of course know that he would never return to England, but nevertheless he sensed that his departure marked a clear end to something. Alongside this sense of bridges burned and (a non-existent) Paradise Lost, perhaps the most important fact of the retrospectively crucial summer of 1816 is Byron's friendship with the poet Percy Bysshe Shelley. Only Byron's arrival in Italy the same autumn and his stay in Venice are as significant for his poetic development.

Percy Shelley and his young second wife Mary, the daughter of the radical thinker William Godwin and the equally radical feminist Mary Wollstonecraft, were travelling in the company of Mary's half-sister Claire Clairmont, who shortly before their departure from England had become one of Byron's lovers. Indeed, Claire knew by the time her party arrived at Geneva, shortly before Byron's, that she was pregnant. The Shelleys took a house at Montalègre, very near Cologny. Although Byron was more than somewhat wary of Claire's intentions, the two households spent much time together (thus incidentally providing more scandal for other English tourists to feed back to Britain). Famously it was a joint ghost-story writing competition, to pass the time in the bad weather, which led to Mary's writing *Frankenstein*.

Despite the presence of a sort of amanuensis in the person of Byron's doctor, John Polidori, it is an irritating fact that little of the substance of the two poets' conversations is recorded. But the mutual influence is obvious in general terms, if difficult to pin down in detail. Shelley gave Byron a great deal of Wordsworth to read, or read it to him, in which a sense of unity with Nature redeemed man's isolation. It would appear he also made him think about the power of the human mind over the circumstances of life. For Shelley, a change in mental attitude could change the whole tenor of life. Although Byron was never able to take this in the almost literal way that Shelley at his most optimistic maintained, it did give him a way of filling the vacuum that human freedom itself seemed to open up beneath him.

Byron was finally to reject Shelley's Wordsworth, which he felt was too systematic an 'answer' to the problem of selfhood, but he transformed some part of Shelley's idealist philosophy into his own version of individualism. The poets can almost be thought of as having a dialogue in their work during this period. *Manfred*, already influenced by Shelley, is answered by Shelley's more optimistic but also less modern dramatic poem *Prometheus Unbound* – less modern because, unlike Byron's poem, a change in the hero's mind-set produces an absolute and not a personal transformation. This dialogue on the individual's power to shape his own life, and/or life at large, was to continue until Shelley's death in 1822.

During this packed summer Byron also met Madame de Staël, an early user of the term Romantic to describe a cultural movement, at her home in Coppet, and with her one of the leaders of the early German Romantics, August Schlegel. We know he also read some of August's brother Friedrich's critical work, and was read some of Goethe's *Faust* (an obvious though not a determining influence on *Manfred*). At Coppet too he met the Abbé di Breme, who plied him with Italian nationalist fervour. A trip round Lake Geneva by boat with Shelley, foreshadowing in an eerie way their later (for Shelley fatal) fascination with boats in Italy, saw them visit sites associated with Rousseau and with Gibbon. Byron had of course moved in literary circles in London – he even went to Coleridge's lectures for example – but there was an intensity about his cultural experience in Switzerland, magnified by his isolation from other society and by the presence of Shelley, which was new.

Alongside this, he was continually reminded of the domestic tragedy in England, and irritated by what he saw as the domestic farce of Claire's infatuation. Although he was out of the pressure-cooker of London fame, he was in the little lakeside community still living in an emotional hot-house. He could not, even during his tour of the Bernese Alps, as he wrote in a journal he kept for Augusta, 'for one moment...lose my own wretched identity'. Shelley's party left for London on 29 August 1816, just three days after Hobhouse arrived to join his friend on their Bernese tour. Byron would never directly communicate with Claire again, though he had ample opportunity to do so in Italy. Back from his inspiring Alpine tour, but now less certain that Venice would be any kind of 'destination', and with a growing feeling that he was to wander for the rest of his days, Byron set off for Italy in early October.

6

Childe Harold III; Manfred

The third canto of *Childe Harold* and the dramatic poem *Manfred* mark the high point of Byron's involvement with the Haroldian 'Byronic' hero. Both offer an exploration rather than a simple dramatization of the existential problems of individuality. But in *Manfred* there is an almost systematic analysis and a decisive turn in the thought process, new enough to stand as a marker for a significant shift in Western sensibility (because of this Byron is, for example, the only poet to have a chapter to himself in Russell's *History of Western Philosophy*).

From the outset, unlike the previous cantos, *Childe Harold* III is aware of its own process. The person who has come to understand life, the narrator tells us in stanza 6, knows why we write poetry:

> 'Tis to create, and in creating live
> A being more intense, that we endow
> With form our fancy, gaining as we give
> The life we image, even as I do now.
> What am I? Nothing; but not so art thou,
> Soul of my thought! with whom I traverse earth,
> Invisible but gazing, as I glow
> Mix'd with thy spirit, blended with thy birth,
> And feeling still with thee in my crush'd feeling's dearth

(*CH*III.6)

Art is the answer to ennui. The process which had been the vehicle for the melodrama of Cantos I and II becomes the subject of this stanza in III. The created character gives meaning to the futile life of its author. This is a significant moment – it can usefully be contrasted to the thought of the draft version of 'Sun of the Sleepless' entitled 'Harmodia' and discussed above in chapter 4. There, art was invariably a diminished copy of life, since expression was always merely a defective copy of the real thing. But here expression is true creation, adding value to a life which is intrinsically worthless. Moreover, when published, the wider resonance of 'Sun of the Sleepless' was unexplored, since the self-conscious exploration of its theme was excised from the lyric. But in this stanza Byron has no such qualms. It is now perfectly reasonable to discuss in a poem the psychology of writing the poem. There is thus both an increase in self-awareness and an increase in the value of self-awareness – to be self-aware is not only a burden, but a way to the lightening of the burden.

Perhaps it would be more accurate to say that 'at the outset', rather than 'from the outset', Canto III is 'aware of its own processes', for this awareness is often forgotten. The characteristic structure of the canto is an oscillation between a desire for the absorption of the burdensome self in an all-embracing nature, and a refusal of that absorption as a mere escape from responsibility. This refusal is imaged either as a sense of how the self's freedom would be compromised by absorption, or more simply as a scepticism that the self could ever be so absorbed. More often than not, the poem seems unaware of this recurring oscillation. This oscillation then is its form, but not its content.

> I live not in myself, but I become
> Portion of that around me; and to me
> High mountains are a feeling, but the hum
> Of human cities torture; I can see
> Nothing to loathe in nature, save to be
> A link reluctant in a fleshly chain,
> Class'd among creatures, when the soul can flee,
> And with the sky, the peak, the heaving plain
> Of ocean, or the stars, mingle, and not in vain.

> And thus I am absorb'd, and this is life:
> I look upon the peopled desart past,
> As on a place of agony and strife,
> Where, for some sin, to Sorrow I was cast,
> To act and suffer, but remount at last
> With a fresh pinion; which I feel to spring,
> Though young, yet waxing vigorous, as the blast
> Which it would cope with, on delighted wing,
> Spurning the clay-cold bonds which round our being cling.

.   .   .   .

Are not the mountains, waves, and skies, a part
Of me and of my soul, as I of them?
Is not the love of these deep in my heart
With a pure passion? should I not contemn
All objects, if compared with these? and stem
A tide of suffering, rather than forego
Such feelings for the hard and worldly phlegm
Of those whose eyes are only turn'd below,
Gazing upon the ground, with thoughts which dare not glow?

But this is not my theme; and I return
To that which is immediate, and require
Those who find contemplation in the urn,
To look on One, whose dust was once all fire,
A native of the land where I respire
The clear air for a while . . .

(CHIII.72–3, 75–6, 1–6)

The Wordsworthian influence is clear, but it is not so much a
literary influence as a genuinely philosophical one. The real
'source' of the thought is the 'One' of stanza 76, the philosopher
Rousseau, whom Byron associates with Lake Geneva (Lac
Leman). Human isolation can be overcome by a realization of
man's place in the Natural Universe. But much more like
Rousseau than Wordsworth, Byron gives a characteristically
morbid spin to his pantheism. To be able to 'feel' and not merely
to 'see' with the physical senses is a common Romantic
aspiration (compare Coleridge's 'Dejection Ode', where the
speaker regrets that he only 'See[s], not feel[s]' the beauty of the
sunset). The narrator here however will only be able to 'feel'
rather than merely 'see' the world when he is dead, when 'dust
is as it should be'. If 'dust' is merely 'dust', the pantheistic point
is somewhat lost. The intense hatred of the physical sours the
picture of the physical beauty around him. It is almost as if it is
the mind which is the problem – there will be peace only when
'dust is as it should be', and the striving for immortality is over,
though this is not what the poem says. Physical nature is better
than man: but is it because it is 'clay' or because it is *not* 'clay'?
We assume the poem to mean because unlike man it is its own
proper element and therefore spiritual, but the thought is
confused if we inspect it closely. How too, are we supposed to
read the successive question marks of stanza 75? Are they

rhetorical, or real? Do they intensify the perception that man is 'a part' of the 'mountains, waves, and skies', or does their increasing intensity ask a real question? If there is an answer at all it must come in the next stanza's turn to human mortality – the 'urn' – and the answer must be 'no'. Transcendence is not the 'theme', mortality is. This rapid downshift from pantheistic desire to mortal reality, in which even the desire is contaminated by its own urgency, is the typical experience of the canto.

Another version of Byron's struggle with the relationship between the individual and the world around can be found in a later passage which seems to echo the list of natural features in stanza 75:

> Sky, mountains, river, winds, lake, lightnings! ye!
> With night, and cloud, and thunder, and a soul
> To make these felt and feeling, well may be
> Things that have made me watchful; the far roll
> Of your departing voices, is the knoll
> Of what in me is sleepless, – if I rest.
> But where of ye, oh tempests! is the goal?
> Are ye like those with the human breast?
> Or do ye find, at length, like eagles, some high nest?
>
> Could I embody and unbosom now
> That which is most within me, – could I wreak
> My thoughts upon expression, and thus throw
> Soul, heart, mind, passions, feelings, strong or weak,
> All that I would have sought, and all I seek,
> Bear, know, feel and yet breathe – into *one* word,
> And that one word were Lightning, I would speak;
> But as it is, I live and die unheard,
> With a most voiceless thought, sheathing it as a sword.

> (CHIII.96–7)

Here the connection with Nature is anything but Wordsworthian, first appearances notwithstanding. The sublime nature of the Alps is like the human spirit, rather than the other way round, and its energy may even be as pointless. The desire is a desire for absoluteness – the 'one' word which would be everything – a return to the usage of 'one' we saw in *Childe Harold* I and II, but now explained, rather than merely a device to tempt the reader's own desire for explanation. The failure of this desire for absolute expression mirrors the failure in the draft version of 'Sun of the Sleepless'.

In Canto III, then, Byron can still be found pushing the extreme individualism, together with its corollary, the sense of failure, which we have found in his earlier work. Romantic Man aspires to Universality, and lives in a consequent agony of failure and futility when self-judged by this absolute standard. He can only struggle on (like the tempest with no rest) or withdraw totally ('I live and die unheard'). This Romantic–tragic attitude also undercuts the attempts to see man in a universal context, a context genuinely larger than the individual.

It is difficult in this unstable canto to speak of progression or development. Nevertheless, when the canto returns to its opening subject, and thus signals its end, it is tempting to look for shifts in attitude which might suggest that the canto has 'helped' the narrator clarify his world-view. The canto (the ostensible subject of which is Byron's journey into exile from Belgium down the Rhine and into Switzerland) is framed by stanzas to his daughter. It is his separation from her which stands as the image of man's alienated existence and introduces the theme, and it is his distant blessing on her which provides at least some kind of resolution. If there is a signal that this is possible, it comes in stanza 114, just before he reintroduces his daughter and the poem's envoi:

> I have not loved the world, nor the world me, –
> But let us part fair foes; I do believe,
> Though I have found them not, that there may be
> Words which are things, – hopes which will not deceive,
> And virtues which are merciful, nor weave
> Snares for the failing; I would also deem
> O'er others' griefs that some sincerely grieve;
> That two, or one, are almost what they seem, –
> That goodness is no name, and happiness no dream.
>
> (CHIII.114)

It is the provisionality of belief here which is the possible key. The narrator appears not to believe that he will find the stability of value he seeks, an absolute quality, and yet is prepared to act out of a residual belief nevertheless. This compromise, this lowering of the sights, perhaps allows relationships to exist on other than absolute levels. It is possible of course to read this stanza in the tones of bitterest irony and cynicism. Just as the stanza if read positively however makes the transition to the sad but loving envoi a smoother one, so the envoi makes it more difficult to read this stanza wholly cynically. In stanza 112 too there is a hint that Byron may be beginning to see past the feeling that anything less than All is Nothing:

> And for these words, thus woven into song,
> It may be that they are a harmless wile, –
> The colouring of the scenes which fleet along,
> Which I would seize, in passing, to beguile
> My breast, or that of others, for a while.
> Fame is the thirst of youth, – but I am not
> So young as to regard men's frown or smile,
> As loss or guerdon of a glorious lot;
> I stood and stand alone, – remembered or forgot.
>
> (CHIII.112)

Art here passes the time – provides the colour, the sense of significance to life, but does not come with the pretensions of religious revelation. Is this significantly different from stanza 6 with which we began our account of the poem? If we simply interpret the two stanzas, perhaps not – art gives meaning to life. But if we are attentive to the tone of the two passages, there is a considerable difference. In the earlier the creativity is Promethean; in the later stanza it is more like a man with a sketch-book and watercolours. It is tempting, and almost necessary if we are to give a consistent account of Byron's development, to see this kind of shift taking place in Canto III. But the truth is that the experience of reading the canto is one of repeated variations on a turbulent theme, rather than any sense of clarifying progression.

In sharp contrast, *Manfred* has an architectural clarity of structure. The format has an almost morality-play feel to it. Byron strenuously but probably disingenuously denied ever having read Marlowe's *Faustus*, to which the first version of *Manfred* bears a very striking resemblance. There are a series of 'temptations', which the hero successfully overcomes, and a 'curse', which he learns to live with. The 'tempters' seek to provide explanations for Manfred's life. His life is predestined, and therefore he has no responsibility for it (shades of Calvin here); his problem is self-consciousness, solvable either by suicide or the almost equivalent retreat to a pastoral backwater;

he should lose himself in the beauty of Nature (the Words-worthian temptation we have already discussed in *Childe Harold,* Canto III); he should sign a Faustian pact with the Satanic powers; he should embrace orthodox religion. All of these 'temptations' he rejects, because although they may soothe the agony of selfhood, they will also compromise his freedom. Freedom and self are for Manfred two sides, positive and negative respectively, of the same coin. The curse is pronounced by Astarte – a figure who, it is pretty clearly implied, is Manfred's sister, and the object of an incestuous passion – and the curse is irredeemable selfhood. The incest motif becomes a sign for the isolation of the self – love is only love-of-self transposed. As the play ends, Manfred is sought by the conventional Faust-play devils, who intend to drag him off to hell. But he refuses to go. It is a quite extraordinary moment. Manfred, a human, isolated, self, refuses to acknowledge the power of any agency outside that self. He is cursed by the isolation and alienation of selfhood, but so be it – that is what it is to be human.

> *Spirit*   Reluctant mortal!
>
>   .   .   .   .
>
>   ... Can it be that thou
> Art thus in love with life? the very life
> That made thee wretched?
> *Manfred*   Thou false fiend, thou liest!
> My life is in its last hour, – *that* I know,
> Nor would redeem a moment of that hour;
> I do not combat against death, but thee,
> And thy surrounding angels...
>
>   .   .   .   .
>
>   ... I stand
> Upon my strength – I do defy – deny –
> Spurn back, and scorn ye! –
> *Spirit*   But thy many crimes
> Have made thee –
> *Manfred*   What are they to such as thee?
> Must crimes be punish'd but by other crimes,
> And greater criminals? – Back to thy hell!
> Thou hast no power upon me, *that* I feel;
> Thou never shalt possess me, *that* I know:
> What I have done is done; I bear within

44

A torture which could nothing gain from thine:
The mind which is immortal makes itself
Requital for its good or evil thoughts –
Is its own origin of ill and end –
And its own place and time – its innate sense,
When stripp'd of this mortality, derives
No colour from the fleeting things without,
But is absorb'd in sufferance or in joy,
Born from the knowledge of its own desert.
Thou didst not tempt me, and thou couldst not tempt me;
I have not been thy dupe, nor am thy prey –
But was my own destroyer, and will be
My own hereafter. – Back, ye baffled fiends!
The hand of death is on me – but not yours!

The Demons disappear

(*Manfred*, III.iv. 104–13, 119–41)

Although it is not so simple, it is tempting to say that this defines the beginning of Byron's maturity. The self is an insoluble problem. Only by recourse to agencies, or systems, outside himself can the individual hope to resolve the problems and tensions within. But these resolutions are as much escape as solution. If the self is valued, it has to remain itself – free, and able to evaluate its own existence. Only the individual has the right of judgement over himself – but with that right comes an obligation, because failure to exercise judgement plunges us into nothingness. If Manfred rejects the devils, he has to substitute himself in their role, or else his life is meaningless. This moment, which might seem like the apotheosis of the Romantic or Byronic self, in fact marks a significant shift away from the idea of the self as rooted in opposition, towards the more modern idea of the self as self-creator. Manfred finds it easy to die now he has assumed responsibility for his life. This repose – 'Old Man, 'tis not so very difficult to die' – is very different from the 'Victory' made of Death at the end of *Prometheus*. But the last words of the play are not even his. They belong to the representative of orthodox religion, the Abbot addressed by Manfred as 'old man', who can only restate the puzzle of mortality, now that the psyche which controlled the meaning of that mortal life has gone. This also marks an important anti-Romantic thread in Byron's later thought. The self controls its own meaning, but it is remorselessly subject to

45

the laws of physical nature. Man creates meaning, but not the physical world. Consciousness gone, meaning too is gone.

> *Abbot* He's gone – his soul hath ta'en its earthless flight –
> Whither? I dread to think – but he is gone.

> (*Manfred*, III.iv.152–3)

Despite its clarity of structure and almost syllogistic conclusion, *Manfred* is still in many ways a product of the same poetic method as *Childe Harold*. One of Byron's 'set-piece' Romantic descriptions appears in the last Act, as Manfred remembers an evening in the Coliseum in Rome:

> The stars are forth, the moon above the tops
> Of the snow-shining mountains. – Beautiful!
> I linger yet with Nature, for the night
> Hath been to me a more familiar face
> Than that of man; and in her starry shade
> Of dim and solitary loveliness,
> I learn'd the language of another world.
> I do remember me, that in my youth,
> When I was wandering – upon such a night
> I stood within the Coloseum's wall,
> 'Midst the chief relics of almighty Rome;
> The trees which grew along the broken arches
> Waved dark in the blue midnight, and the stars
> Shone through the rents of ruin; from afar
> The watchdog bayed beyond the Tiber; and
> More near from out the Caesars' palace came
> The owl's long cry, and, interruptedly,
> Of distant sentinels the fitful song
> Begun and died upon the gentle wind.

> (*Manfred*, III.iv.1–19)

There is no very good reason for this passage being there (Manfred's excuse that the mind wanders at moments of crisis reads almost as Byron's excuse for putting in a passage with no relevance – he has just visited Rome), except in so far as it monumentalizes the hero by association with that which he is describing. Much the same can be said of the description of the setting sun a little earlier in the same Act. The effect of the passage is to identify the hero with a transcendent body. Manfred addresses the sun:

> Thou material God!

– and then identifies with his setting:

> ...He is gone:
> I follow.

(Manfred, III.ii.14, 29–30)

This poetic technique implies nearly the opposite message from that which *Manfred* as a whole spells out so clearly, for it relies on the supra-human to give value to the human. There is an even odder example at the crucial moment of Manfred's rejection of the devils:

> The mind which is immortal makes itself
> Requital for its good or evil thoughts –
> Is its own origin of ill and end –
> And its own place and time...

(Manfred, III.iv.129–32)

This is a close paraphrase of Satan in Milton's *Paradise Lost*, Book 1. For a moment it reinstates the politics of opposition – as if Manfred is an ally of the rebel Satan – at precisely the moment when this common Romantic position is being superseded. Manfred is not restating the Haroldian position, but the rhetoric of his poem frequently does – isolation is painful but heroic, and there is a moral imperative to oppose the unopposable. Byron does not yet have at his disposal a revolutionary form for his new position, and yet again we are not dealing with a simplistic linear development. Nevertheless, in hindsight it is possible to see *Manfred* as the hinge point in Byron's career, and that not only because of its convenient chronology.

47

7

Exile in Italy: Rebuilding a Life

In Milan Byron renewed his acquaintance with the Abbé di Breme, who now more seriously educated him into Italian politics. In di Breme's circle he also met the writer Stendhal, who had been one of Napoleon's secretaries. Byron had always associated Napoleon with the radical side of the French Revolution, as an anti-establishment figure rather than an aspirant emperor. Not that he was blind to the bloodshed that had followed in Napoleon's wake, but when pushed he would identify with the foe of the English establishment and of European monarchies. It was easy then for him to have sympathies with the nationalist group in which he now found himself, who were opposed to the imposition of Austrian rule over Lombardy and Piedmont following the settlements after Napoleon's defeat at Waterloo. For Byron this was simply the re-establishment of the ancien régime. His association with this group did not go unnoticed by the Austrian authorities, particularly after an incident in La Scala Opera House, in which Polidori managed to have himself arrested, and Byron and his companions had to give their names to have him released. From this point on, Byron was under the almost totally incompetent surveillance of the Austrian secret police.

Hobhouse and Byron moved on to Venice in November. Here the effects of the Austrian occupation were felt if anything even more directly, and Byron was made to feel acutely conscious of England's role in the peace settlement. He began to speak seriously of never returning to England. He found the atmosphere of Venice extremely congenial, and, of course, its relaxed sexual mores were much to his taste. These latter, it should be noted, though recognizing the fact of sexual appetite which English society attempted to pretend was narrowly controllable, were not an out-and-out charter of free love, but had their own rules of behaviour. He studied Venetian dialect, and Armenian at the monastery in the Lagoon. He began an affair with Marianna Segati, the wife of his landlord, and entered into the Carnival festivities with zest, though it was the Carnival of the following year that left him 'debilitated' with a social disease for a few weeks. He writes continuously to his friends, notably the Irish poet Tom Moore, full of admiration for Venice, but sometimes speculating on a return to England if there should be a political revolution, and sometimes too complaining that his life still seemed a directionless exile, filled only by the bitterness of the separation.

Hobhouse had long since returned to England leaving his friend isolated but relatively contented in an almost domestic setting with Marianna, when Byron finally summoned the energy to set off on a tour to Bologna, Florence and Rome. It is this trip, together with his first experience of Venice, which forms the basis of *Childe Harold* Canto IV. On the journey he begins to wonder what to do about his daughter by Claire, provisionally called Alba (Dawn) by Shelley, but finally called Allegra. The incidence of names beginning with 'A' in Byron's female relations is striking, as we have already noted, and it might, or might not, lie behind the names of the last two heroines of *Don Juan*, Adeline and Aurora (which also means Dawn). By the time he returns to Venice, and his relationship with Marianna, he is taking active measures to put his affairs in England in an order which will allow him to live permanently abroad. By this time too the revised third Act of *Manfred*, written under the influence of his reading of the sceptical Voltaire, had been sent to his publisher, and Byron moved out of Venice for the summer, to a rented palace on the river Brenta at La Mira known as the Villa Foscarini. It was here that Marianna's husband, visiting a lover of his own who lived nearby, told Byron the story that was shortly to form the basis of *Beppo*. This happily coincided with a visit by an English acquaintance, bringing books (and tooth-powder), who happened also to be a friend of John Hookham Frere, a poet who had used the Italian ottava rima verse form in English. *Beppo*, the first of the major poems in this form, the poems which modern critics believe to be his greatest achievements, was underway.

This late summer of 1817 finds Byron, then, in a new mood of calm, or, when thinking of his past life, at least of resignation. He has in Italy the freedom of an outsider, and yet he has a recognized place in a small group of people. He has sexual freedom, and yet this not in a spirit of rebellion, but as part of an accepted social system. Moreover, as a sympathetic representative of a major European power, he is made to feel he has some purchase on the political situation, whereas in England he may have been famous but he was made to feel powerless by the party system. The summer of 1816 was the end of the beginning. This late summer of 1817 is the beginning of his new life. The seal was set when in December he received news that Newstead Abbey was finally sold.

Early in 1818 Byron rented the Palazzo Mocenigo on the Grand Canal. He had also rented another house on the Brenta which he invited Shelley to use. Meantime, Shelley had brought Allegra (and Claire, whom Byron refused to see) with him, and Allegra moved in with Byron – and a whole menagerie of animals which the poet kept – in the Palazzo Mocenigo. This arrangement was unlikely to last, not so much because of Byron's views of the matter, but because of the intervention of a whole litany of those who thought they were acting in Allegra's best interests, not least the Shelleys, and, more justifiably, her mother. It was all later to end in tragedy, when Allegra, sent to a convent by Byron as much to rid himself of her would-be protectors as anything, died of a fever. But this again was a period in which Shelley and Byron saw a good deal of each other – Shelley's poem *Julian and Maddalo* is based on these meetings – and it was now that Byron first announced his work on *Don Juan*.

Two threads remain to be picked up in Byron's stay in Italy, and though they are interwoven, we will deal only with one in this chapter – his long-term affair with the Countess Guiccioli. His involvement in Italian politics we save until chapter 9.

He met Teresa Guiccioli in Venice in the spring of 1819 (they had actually been briefly introduced the year before), and remained involved with her until his departure for Greece in 1823. Teresa was of course from a different class than his earlier extended Italian affairs, and had a powerful but ageing husband. During the course of their relationship this marriage broke down, given a distinct push by Teresa's radical father Count Gamba, who appealed directly to the Pope to grant a separation. Teresa from this point on had to live with her relations, which might have been better than with her husband, but actually restricted the lovers' meetings even more initially. It was not until 1822 that she and Byron lived under the same roof in Pisa. It was a peripatetic few years – but that was nothing new for Byron – seeing relative rest in Ravenna, Pisa, and finally Genoa. What was new was a relationship, increasingly as the years went by on a daily domestic basis, lasting for four years. Throughout this period, and despite occasional attempts by Teresa to have him abandon it, Byron was at work on *Don Juan*.

It is tempting to read these last Italian years as autumnal – rich but also somehow a harbinger of departure. For Byron all mortal commitment was inevitably provisional, but the continual realization of that provisionality consumed a vast amount of energy, and perhaps even Byron's energy was not infinite. If in 1823 he preferred rendering his commitment to Teresa relative in the face of the higher demands of politics, he had no illusions about the nature of the politics to which he was 'provisionally' committing himself. And yet commitment was something he no longer had the energy perhaps to resist. Though Teresa idolized her life with Byron, it had, as most domestic relationships have, as many downs as ups. But it can be said to have survived, and its survival is readable in the great poem whose birth accompanied it.

8

Childe Harold **IV**; *Beppo; Don Juan; The Vision of Judgment*

CHILDE HAROLD IV

Byron had called *Manfred* 'mental theatre', and his most 'metaphysical' piece. It certainly abandoned completely his concern for the everyday, and yet the conclusion it reached was to plunge its writer back into the very real world. It does not announce the death of metaphysics, since that remains one of the main human ways of thinking about our lives, but it certainly comes close. At the very least, metaphysics must always be aware that it is a human creation. In Italy Byron was to find a literary model which could carry this new world view without the contradictions we have discussed in *Manfred*. The key driving force was the realization that meaning was 'artificially' produced – that it was a product, not of nature or a supernatural being, but of man and his civilization. This leads Byron in his later years first to adopt the highly contrived Italian verse form known as ottava rima, and secondly to espouse a rigidly classical view of dramatic construction. Both of these developments saw him prefer neoclassical models of poetry to what (when he learned of the term) he called the Romantic, in disparaging tones. And the final canto of *Childe Harold*, though retaining the verse form of the earlier cantos and some of their mannerisms, is also coloured by this new palette.

The 'pilgrim's shrine' of Canto IV is now not Greece, but Rome. While this is obviously simply a reflection of where the poet himself happened to be, its cultural significance is highlighted by the texture of the poem. Whereas Greece defined the borders of civilization and nature in terms of a natural civilization, Rome represents civilization as art. Saint Peter's and the statues of the Vatican are 'the fountain of sublimity', and from them (in a very eighteenth-century phrase) man may 'learn what great conceptions can'. Italy is the country of Dante, Petrarch, Ariosto, and Tasso. If Byron identifies with the human struggles of these figures (particularly Tasso) in ways which accentuate their Haroldian qualities (isolation, political oppression, exile from love), they are also figures who have succeeded in enriching human life.

The politics of opposition does remain:

Yet, Freedom! yet thy banner, torn, but flying,
Streams like the thunder-storm *against* the wind;
Thy trumpet voice, though broken now and dying,
The loudest still the tempest leaves behind;
Thy tree hath lost its blossoms, and the rind,
Chopp'd by the axe, looks rough and little worth,
But the sap lasts, – and still the seed we find
Sown deep, even in the bosom of the North;
So shall a better spring less bitter fruit bring forth.

(CHIV.98)

And indeed the picture of the death of the gladiator is an archetypal Romantic–Byronic moment:

I see before me the Gladiator lie:
He leans upon his hand – his manly brow
Consents to death, but conquers agony,
And his drooped head sinks gradually low –
And through his side the last drops, ebbing slow
From the red gash, fall heavy, one by one,
Like the first of a thunder-shower; and now
The arena swims around him – he is gone,
Ere ceased the inhuman shout which hail'd the wretch who won.

He heard it, but he heeded not – his eyes
Were with his heart, and that was far away;
He reck'd not of the life he lost nor prize,
But where his rude hut by the Danube lay
There were his young barbarians all at play,
There was their Dacian mother – he, their sire,
Butcher'd to make a Roman holiday –

All this rush'd with his blood – Shall he expire
And unavenged? – Arise! ye Goths, and glut your ire!

(CHIV.140–1)

Alienation, futile death, political oppression – they are all there in a 'frozen', monumental picture worthy of any Turkish Tale. But along with these scenes of dramatized despair runs a tougher view of the duties of creativity:

Of its own beauty is the mind diseased,
And fevers into false creations: – where,
Where are the forms the sculptor's soul hath seized?
In him alone. Can Nature shew so fair?
Where are the charms and virtues which we dare
Conceive in boyhood and pursue as men,
The unreach'd Paradise of our despair,
Which o'er-informs the pencil and the pen,
And overpowers the page where it would bloom again?

(CHIV.122)

There has been a radical shift since 'Harmodia'. The artist no longer creates a poor copy – he creates the only original. And although this is not what Man wants – he wants a *real* ideal – this is all there is. *Childe Harold* IV gives many reasons for this state of affairs, sometimes sounding as if life at root is contingent, sometimes as if it is the consequence of original sin. But the duty to create, against all the odds, is consistent:

Yet let us ponder boldly – 'tis a base
Abandonment of reason to resign
Our right of thought – our last and only place
Of refuge; this, at least, shall still be mine:
Though from our birth the faculty divine
Is chain'd and tortured – cabin'd, cribb'd, confined,
And bred in darkness, lest the truth should shine
Too brightly on the unprepared mind,
The beam pours in, for time and skill will couch [= to cure a
    cataract] the blind.

(CHIV.127)

At the end of the canto (in stanzas 178–184) the narrator returns to the ocean as the image of eternity, a Nature which, at first rather Wordsworthian, then sublimely indifferent to Man, has also at least one of his qualities – his isolation – 'thou goest forth, dread, fathomless, alone'. This word 'alone' seems to trigger in the next stanza a new approach to nature. It is not an absorber of the self, nor yet a cold physical materiality, but almost an equal:

> And I have loved thee, Ocean! And my joy
> Of youthful sports was on thy breast to be
> Borne, like thy bubbles, onward; from a boy
> I wantoned with thy breakers – they to me
> Were a delight; and if the freshening sea
> Made them a terror – 'twas a pleasing fear,
> For I was as it were a child of thee,
> And trusted to thy billows far and near,
> And laid my hand upon thy mane – as I do here.

(CHIV.184)

There is also in this stanza a new physical immediacy – 'as I do here'. This low-key immediacy, quite in keeping with the canto's often up-to-the-minute social concerns (the death of Princess Charlotte in child-birth for example), introduces a note of the personal more akin to the '[Epistle to Augusta]' than to the bitter but stylized invective against those Byron feels have driven him from England (in particular of course his wife). The two stanzas which follow this and which close the poem, full of the mock-archaisms of Canto I – 'sandal-shoon and scallop-shell' – and of the dramatization of failure, seem an almost deliberate tossing of the old manner to the winds. Byron wrote the concluding stanzas sometime in the early summer of 1817, but by the time the canto was 'finished' on 7 January 1818, Byron was within twelve days of sending *Beppo* (begun in October 1817) to his publisher. The 'ottava rima' period had begun.

BEPPO

The story-line of *Beppo*, once unravelled from the many digressions which interrupt it, is simple. Beppo has been so long away from his wife Laura and his Venetian home on a trading voyage that Laura presumes he is dead. On the day of the action Laura and her lover, the Count, are at a Carnival ball. On the way home to Laura's house, they are followed by a strange-looking Turk. At the door the 'Turk' reveals himself – Beppo in disguise. In order to avoid a public scene the Count invites him into the house, Beppo's own home of course, and instead of a duel, or at the least explanations and apologies, Laura launches into an inquisition on the manners of the Turks, how she looks, how Beppo looks, will he give her the shawl he's wearing, and all kinds of trivia. As the poem ends, the hint is that they settle down to a more or less comfortable *ménage à trois*. If there is a moral to the story, it is that we cannot say farewell to the flesh ('Carnival'), but must tolerate and compromise with its foibles. It is in our power to turn this possibly sorry state of affairs into an amusing story – to make our life worthwhile at best, or pass the time at worst. The bones of this story were told to Byron and his friend Hobhouse by the husband of Byron's own lover of the time – and its message in that context was clear, much to Hobhouse's horror and Byron's amusement.

But the adoption of ottava rima and various other devices mean that the implications of *Beppo* are much wider than even a plea for tolerance. Let us look first at the stanza form, which is the basis also of *Don Juan* and *The Vision of Judgment*. We have seen the basic outline already in [Epistle to Augusta] – the rhyme scheme ABABABCC – difficult in English, and easily made to sound artificial if the syntax coincides with the line ending – that is, if the rhymes are in any way emphasized. In [Epistle] Byron goes to some length to downplay the rhyme (for example, eleven of the sixteen stanzas have an enjambement leading the reader over the end of the first line of the stanza into the second line, and thus blurring the rhyme word which gives the clue to the stanza's 'a' rhyme). In *Beppo* the tactic is the opposite – the rhymes are usually highlighted. What general effect does this have (we will look at more specific effects in our consideration of *Don Juan*)?

The reader is continually made aware that she/he is reading poetry. This is not a transparent 'window on the world', but something which has been 'put together'. It is a work of art. It is a work of civilization, not a given of Nature. To the same end, Byron constantly explicitly reminds the reader of the nature of what he is reading – the poem is self-reflexive – it tells us about its own composition. For example, here is our introduction to Laura:

> A certain lady went to see the show,
> Her real name I know not, nor can guess,

> And so we'll call her Laura, if you please,
> Because it slips into my verse with ease.
>
> (*Beppo*, 21. 5–8)

But it is not just the jokey reference to the difficulties of rhyming which is self-reflexive here – the name Laura has been very deliberately chosen for its previous history in literature. Laura was the unattainable love of Petrarch, one of Byron's poetic heroes. But Beppo's Laura is all too attainable. This introduces us to another of Byron's devices in the ottava rima poems – constant oblique referral to other literature ('intertextuality'), usually with the aim of a surprising shift of context. What has been thought of as a fixed point of literary history is suddenly given a rude push, and shown to be movable after all. All meaning is human, and can therefore be changed. This 'mortality' of meaning may be depressing, but it is also itself the source of new meanings, and new life. The poem is soaked in 'cultural' reference. To art:

> They've pretty faces yet, those same Venetians,
> Black eyes, arch'd brows, and sweet expressions still,
> Such as of old were copied from the Grecians,
> In ancient arts by moderns mimick'd ill;
> And like so many Venuses of Titian's
> (The best's at Florence – see it, if ye will)
> They look when leaning over the balcony,
> Or stepp'd from out a picture by Giorgione,
>
> Whose tints are truth and beauty at their best;
> And when you to Manfrini's palace go,
> That picture (howsoever fine the rest)
> Is loveliest to my mind of all the show;
> It may perhaps be also to *your* zest,
> And that's the cause I rhyme upon it so...
>
> (*Beppo*, 11–12.1–6)

To literature:

> Shakespeare described the sex in Desdemona
> As very fair, but yet suspect in fame,
> And to this day from Venice to Verona
> Such matters may be probably the same...
>
> (*Beppo*, 17. 1–4)

And to the trivia of contemporary life:

> Ketchup, Soy, Chili-vinegar, and Harvey['s sauce]
>
> *(Beppo*, 8.1.7)

In all of these passages the 'normal' significance of the artefacts is changed, sometimes dramatically, sometimes more subtly. A great painting is also an objective, a trophy, for the tourist; an icon of dramatic literature is in a warped way related to contemporary behaviour; popular sauces become the stuff of poetry. 'Culture' is both a generator of meaning, and trivial artifice. Though in logic contradictory, these two qualities in life coexist. The poem's message of toleration is carried in the same way by the apparently trivial. When the threesome enter Laura's (and Beppo's) house in a state of high tension:

> They entered, and for coffee called, – it came,
> A beverage for Turks and Christians both,
> Although the way they make it's not the same.
>
> *(Beppo*, 91.1–3)

The brotherhood of man, and the common taste for coffee, allow for any number of individual and cultural variations. But the poem does not mention the commonality of the human condition – it only talks about the coffee. The grand idea has gone, and is replaced by the empirical and the material, moulded into meaning by the effort of the story-teller. Laura's inquisitorial tirade which breaks the silence is the apotheosis of trivia (it is precisely avoiding the 'big issue' – the question of marital fidelity, even of revenge), and yet it moulds the end of the poem into toleration, and prevents the grand finale of accusation and duel:

> Now Laura, much recovered, or less loth
> To speak, cries 'Beppo! what's your pagan name?
> Bless me! your beard is of amazing growth!
> And how came you to keep away so long?
> Are you not sensible 'twas very wrong?
>
> 'And are you *really, truly*, now a Turk?
> With any other women did you wive?
> Is't true they use their fingers for a fork?
> Well, that's the prettiest shawl – as I'm alive!
> You'll give it me? They say you eat no pork.
> And how so many years did you contrive
> To – Bless me! did I ever? No, I never
> Saw a man grown so yellow! How's your liver?

'Beppo! that beard of yours becomes you not;
It shall be shaved before you're a day older;
Why do you wear it? Oh! I had forgot –
Pray don't you think the weather here is colder?
How do I look? You shan't stir from this spot
In that queer dress, for fear some beholder
Should find you out, and make the story known.
How short your hair is! Lord! how grey it's grown!'

(*Beppo*, 91.4–93.8)

There is no 'meaning' outside the action, outside the story, outside our story. This low-key version of Manfred's refusal to have anything to do with transcendence leads to a devaluation of endings in general – they no longer 'conclude', 'sum-up' – they merely stop. When the story is over, everything is over. The poem (perhaps accidentally since it grew by accretion, but nevertheless appropriately) ends not on the full-close of a hundredth stanza, but on the ninety-ninth. It ends not climactically, but almost accidentally. And with an optimistic uplift on the final word – 'begun':

Whate'er his youth had suffer'd, his old age
With wealth and talking made him some amends;
Though Laura sometimes put him in a rage,
I've heard the Count and he were always friends.
My pen is at the bottom of a page,
Which being finished, here the story ends;
'Tis to be wished it had been sooner done,
But stories somehow lengthen when begun.

(*Beppo*, 99)

The 'story' in question is not only Beppo's, but life's. The extension of the story is a matter of both skill and accident – Beppo has the ability to tell stories, as has the poem's narrator, but yet the stories also only 'somehow' lengthen. Although we have described the plot of *Beppo* as simple, the narrative structure is anything but simple, being a cat's cradle of digression and digression within digression. The clear route to a goal is not this narrator's way, nor, his method implies, is it life's. The melodrama of absolute failure and isolation is gone; it is replaced by the comedy of gentle effort, compromise, and partial success on a limited scale. Man is freed from an overpowering nostalgia for Paradise.

DON JUAN

If the plot, or anti-plot, of *Beppo* is easy to summarize, the reverse is true of Byron's longest masterpiece, *Don Juan*. Perhaps the best way to think of it is as a human (as opposed to a divine) epic. Byron, under pressure to write a traditional epic, wrote to his publisher from Venice in April 1819:

> So you and Mr Foscolo etc. want me to undertake what you call a 'great work?' an Epic poem I suppose or some such pyramid. – I'll try no such thing – I hate tasks.... And works too! – is Childe Harold nothing? You have so many 'divine' poems is it nothing to have written a Human one? without any of your worn out machinery...– since you want length you shall have enough of Juan for I'll make 50 Cantos...

Don Juan continually invokes and evokes the epic genre in order to distance itself from it. For example:

> Most epic poets plunge in 'medias res,'
> (Horace makes this the heroic turnpike road)
> And then your hero tells, whene'er you please,
> What went before – by way of episode,
> While seated after dinner at his ease,
> Beside his mistress in some soft abode,
> Palace, or garden, paradise, or cavern,
> Which serves the happy couple for a tavern.

> *(DJI.6)*

> Hail, Muse! *et cetera.* – We left Juan sleeping...

> *(DJIII.1)*

Picaresque, with Quixote not very far away, digressive, with Shandy at hand, *Don Juan* paints *Beppo* on a large canvas. One might say on a universal scale, did that not contradict the secularity of its texture. The poem's self-reflexiveness can make it seem very proto-postmodernist, and in many ways this is fair, so long as one is clear about one's understanding of postmodernism. Byron's poem is not merely ludic.

Perhaps the most obvious way of mapping this Protean monster of a poem is to focus on the sequence of love affairs, which are, after all, at the core of the *Don Juan* myth. The social creation of gender can be added to Byron's view of civilization-dependent meaning. *Don Juan* is by and large a passive 'seducer' in Byron's poem, whereas many commentators on the myth, not least Coleridge in his *Biographia Literaria* (1817), which Byron knew, see him as a Promethean figure. But far from the politics of opposition, Juan has to make sense of a world he does not control, and has no wish to control. If we list his affairs – Julia, Haidée, Dudù, Gulbeyaz whom he refuses, Catherine the Great, and finally Fitzfulke, with the much more serious Adeline and Aurora waiting in the wings – the majority have the woman taking the lead, and the rest (bar arguably the night with Dudù) are an equal partnership. Moreover, there is an episode of cross-dressing in the Harem scenes with Gulbeyaz and Dudù in which Juan is disguised as a female (there are earlier incidents in the Turkish Tales of women disguised as men), and not only do Gulbeyaz and Catherine with their royal authority have manly characteristics, but so too does even the simple Haidée, when she defies her father. All this has led a number of critics to see Byron's view of *gender* as modern, socially dependent. This would certainly be entirely consistent with Byron's overall position, as we have seen, but we should also remember that there was a long literary history of cross-dressing which did not have much to do with anti-essentialism. The ambiguities of Byron's own *sexuality* lean heavily of course on any critic in this area, whatever their view.

There is no doubt though, even if we compare Byron's character only to that of Mozart's opera, which he almost certainly knew, that his Don Juan has undergone an inversion, and the more so if we compare him also with Byron's own earlier heroes. Mozart's anti-hero rises to Faustian defiance at the end when the Commendatore's statue comes to life, but Donny Johnny (as Byron sometimes styled him in correspondence) resists the flow of things only under extreme pressure. The poem's instinct is like Laura's in *Beppo* – make the best of things, avoid heroism until the individual's freedom is terminally threatened. But like Manfred the individual's responsibility to himself is the sticking point. Hence Don Juan does refuse Gulbayez (he is at his most 'manly' then when dressed as a woman). In this sense gender is certainly fluid, depending both on circumstance and on individual choice. This is not inconsistent either with Byron's own gender positioning in life. It does not rest on a single quality – we are a long way from that insistence on 'one' defining quality that was such a part of the heroic rhetoric of the earlier poems.

It is tempting to make further sense of the affairs by noting certain symmetries. The most obvious (and made explicit in the poem) is the Haidée/Aurora parallel. Haidée is a child of nature (despite being the daughter of a pirate!) who rescues Juan when he is washed up on the beach after a shipwreck. She is entirely innocent, living on an island which the narrator is at some pains to show is an island 'out of time', and therefore an unsustainable idyll. Her father marches towards the unsuspecting lovers for some full 120 stanzas of suspense. In Aurora's case the suspense (will she and Juan fall in love; is Adeline their hostess plotting against this?) is even longer (over 185 stanzas), and is unresolved at the end of the poem as we have it. And although Aurora cannot be 'Nature's all' as was Haidée, nevertheless she has some of the same unworldliness (see *DJ*XV.58 for example). The next question is what does the reader make of this parallel? Is it simply a shape, another form by which the random repetitions of life can be made to seem meaningful? Or are we supposed to see some kind of teleology, progression, from Haidée in Cantos II, III and IV, to Aurora in XIV, XV, XVI and XVII? There are other possible symmetries at work – Gulbeyaz and Catherine is an obvious one, distinguished by Juan's resistance to one and not to the other. But more questionable and more interesting is a possible parallel between Julia and Adeline, which would then reinforce a strong similarity between the early and late cantos, and might even suggest an overall shape, and an impending conclusion, to the poem. Julia is much more worldly-wise than Haidée, but does not recognize (or chooses not to recognize) her own motivation, when she 'sets up' her own seduction. Adeline is extremely sophisticated, but again does not know 'her own heart' (*DJ*XIV.91), and the hint is clearly that she is in love with Juan. She is clearly plotting something, but whether it is to avoid Juan having an affair with Fitzfulke, or whether it is to avoid him marrying Aurora by *having* an affair with Fitzfulke, and thus remaining 'free', is anybody's guess. The reader is certainly asked to compare Adeline and Aurora (whose names conveniently both begin with the same letter – as did a very significant number of Byron's own significant women – Augusta, Annabella, Ada, Allegra). It is as if the diffuse contrast between Julia and Haidée was now being concentrated in the rerun. What is at stake in this contrast and comparison?

Haidée and Aurora are two versions of the Romantic ideal – natural in Haidée's case, and Paradisical in Aurora's – Aurora is a Catholic, her faith a 'civilized' version of Haidée's instinctive belief. Even in his relativized world, Byron is no cynic. The human desire for absolute purity and faith does not vanish with the knowledge that it is likely to be an illusion. Indeed, it is this desire which motivates human creativity, and thus provides life with what significance it has. On the other hand, Julia and Adeline are two versions of Byronic realism – compromisers, diplomats of the world, but with a residual nostalgia for certainty. It is of Adeline that Byron coins the term 'mobility', often seen as a key description of his own post-*Manfred* work:

> I am not sure that mobility is English, but it is expressive of a quality which rather belongs to other climates, though it is sometimes seen to a great extent in our own. It may be defined as an excessive susceptibility of immediate impressions – at the same time without *losing* the past; and is, though sometimes apparently useful to the possessor, a most painful and unhappy attribute. (Byron's note to *DJ*XVI.97.4)

Because they are under human control, situations and 'truths' change – this does not invalidate what has gone before. To understand this is to acknowledge the relativity of human experience, but this does not plunge us into irredeemable chaos – because we have the desire for the ideal, for shape, for form, for meaning.

So Haidée and Aurora, and Julia and Adeline, become the two pairs of a systole–diastole, the breathing in and the breathing out of human experience. This double view of life can be called Romantic Irony, but Byron's version of it is to be distinguished from that of the German theorists (in particular Friedrich Schlegel) who coined the term. For Byron, unlike the Germans, irony was a process in life, not the truth of life. That there are multiple views of things is how things are, but that perception does not lead to moral superiority. On the other hand, a failure to allow people their own view is morally culpable. Gulbeyaz and Catherine fail in different ways to realize that love is an act of freedom. All the love affairs, and therefore the movement of the poem, circle around this complex kernel.

Byron's poem only becomes unkind to those who seek seriously to control the lives of those around them, and only seriously unkind to those who take that to its logical conclusion. Even then, its toleration goes far, unless the person is acting out some phantasy of ideology – or 'system' as Byron would have said – which denies individual responsibility. Byron's harshest words are reserved for the warmongers in Cantos VII and VIII. But even here Byron is much kinder to Suwarrow the Russian general than he is to Wellington, because the Russian is simply going about his business (and he is rather good at it), whereas Wellington believes he is fighting for the right.

It is important however to remember that the experience of reading *Don Juan* is not an experience of generalities. Given the view of life the poem takes, it would be highly surprising if it were. On the contrary, the texture of the poem is mundane, material, humane, and uses its highly mannered, sophisticated verse form to make even trivia worth reading about. I shall take Canto XV, as a canto of handleable size, as an example. Most of the techniques we shall examine will already be familiar from our discussion of *Beppo*.

Like *Beppo*, Canto XV has ninety-nine stanzas, that oddly nearly-but-not-quite number (a few stanzas were added in the original draft to bring it up to this number). The narrator claims that it begins randomly and ends for the purely mechanical reason that he does not want to write about ghosts at night, so he will postpone the Fitzfulke saga until the following day. Here are the opening stanzas:

> Ah! – What should follow slips from my reflection:
> Whatever follows ne'ertheless may be
> As àpropos of hope or retrospection,
> As though the lurking thought had follow'd free.
> All present life is but an Interjection,
> An 'Oh!' or 'Ah!' of joy or misery,
> Or a 'Ha! ha!' or 'Bah!' – a yawn, or 'Pooh!',
> Of which perhaps the latter is most true.
>
> But, more or less, the whole's a syncopé,
> Or a singultus – emblems of Emotion,
> The grand Antithesis to great Ennui,
> Wherewith we break our bubbles on the ocean,
> That Watery Outline of Eternity,

> Or miniature at least, as is my notion,
> Which ministers unto the soul's delight,
> In seeing matters which are out of sight.
>
> (*DJ*XV.1–2)

Writing – that emblem of emotion – stands against the great ennui; it doesn't really matter what it is about, so long as it's about something. But if it is to be about something, it cannot in fact be completely random, and of course Canto XV has more design than at first appears. Here is the last stanza:

> Between two worlds life hovers like a star,
> 'Twixt night and morn, upon the horizon's verge:
> How little do we know that which we are!
> How less what we may be! The eternal surge
> Of time and tide rolls on, and bears afar
> Our bubbles; as the old burst, new emerge,
> Lash'd from the foam of ages; while the graves
> Of Empires heave but like some passing waves.
>
> (*DJ*XV.99)

Immediately, we notice that Byron has returned to the simile used at the beginning of the canto. This 'random' canto signals its end in the traditional musical way. But the reprise of the simile is of course different from its first occurrence. At the beginning it is highly self-conscious. We are aware that the ocean is an 'emblem', a work of art, an 'outline' or 'miniature'. The term 'miniature' too raises the pitch of the artifice – a small-scale work, probably a copy – and even that only in the judgement of one person ('as is my notion'). But in the last stanza the simile has become 'real'. It *is* the 'eternal surge' of time and tide, it *is* the foam of ages. Byron does not fall into the trap that many postmodernists wallow in – because meaning is created it does not follow that most of the time we *experience* it as created. On the contrary, we experience it as 'given', as 'real'. Even Adeline's 'mobility' is 'real':

> Juan, when he cast a glance
> On Adeline while playing her grand role,
> Which she went through as if it were a dance,
> (Betraying only now and then her soul
> By a look scarce perceptibly askance
> Of weariness or scorn) began to feel
> Some doubt how much of Adeline was *real*;

So well she acted, all and every part
By turns – with that vivacious versatility,
Which many people take for want of heart.
They err – 'tis merely what is called mobility,
A thing of temperament and not of art,
Though seeming so, from its supposed facility;
And false – though true; for surely they're sincerest,
Who are strongly acted on by what is nearest.

(DJXVI. 96.2–8, 97)

Only in the very last phrase of Canto XV does the narrator return to the use of a simile, and not even here to the use of a self-conscious simile – 'heave but like some passing waves'. The graves still really do 'heave' – the simile is still inside as it were the unstated simile or metaphor of 'time' as 'ocean'. The effect of introducing the simile is only further to diminish the Empires – they do not even have the status of 'passing waves', they are only 'like' passing waves. If we return to the second stanza, we will also notice that here the ocean's function as a simile is to allow us 'to see matters which are out of sight'. It is a fine question whether we read this ironically – as it is impossible to see matters which are out of sight, the inference might be that they do not exist. The verse points us in this direction. The off-key rhymes of the second stanza only clarify in the couplet (this as we shall see is the opposite of Byron's more common practice in ottava rima), and this produces a jauntily simplistic feeling, helped by the metrical stress on 'out' – the soul may be 'delighted', but it does not sound as if it has been en-lightened. Precisely this lightly mocked function of vision has vanished in the last stanza. Nothing shows us what is 'out of sight' – we are on the 'horizon's verge', but cannot see over it. As the writing stops for the night, so the literal, the unmeaningful, presses upon us.

Canto XV is exceptional in providing such an obvious overall symmetry in the face of chaos, and thus resisting chaos even as at the end it introduces it 'for real'. But all of Don Juan plays the same game with the stanza form. It is like a chess game, with infinite variations on a fixed theme, set by the conventional rules of the game. The basic process is a circular or oscillating one. The meaning tries to 'break free' from the stanza. If meaning is to fulfil our normal – and Romantic – expectations of it, it should be independent of its physical medium. And the *Don Juan* stanza continually reminds us that it is not. *But* the *Don Juan* stanza continually reminds us that we are not wholly subject to this physical medium either. We can – almost – break free. Anything can be made to mean:

> I perch upon an humbler promontory,
> Amidst life's infinite variety:
> With no great care for what is nicknamed glory,
> But speculating as I cast mine eye
> On what may suit or may not suit my story,
> And never straining hard to versify,
> I rattle on exactly as I'd talk
> With any body in a ride or walk.
>
> I don't know that there may be much ability
> Shown in this sort of desultory rhyme;
> But there's a conversational facility,
> Which may round off an hour upon a time.
> Of this I'm sure at least, there's no servility
> In mine irregularity of chime,
> Which rings what's uppermost of new or hoary,
> Just as I feel the 'Improvisatore.'

(*DJ*XV.19–20)

The first stanza above, self-reflexive as ever, could almost stand as the credo of the poem. Life's 'infinite variety', as opposed to transcendent 'Oneness' is this poem's stuff. Anything in this mundane world can be made to mean, providing you make the creative effort – which does not have to be superhuman. Closer inspection reveals considerable creative effort, and we are supposed to notice it, taking the hint given by the self-reflexive subject. For not only is the polysyllabic 'promontory' welded into the weak rhymes 'glory' and 'story', and not only are we conscious of the pulling of 'variety' into concordance with 'eye' and 'versify', but all of the rhymes before the couplet have some relation to each other. Thus 'eye' is as related to 'promontory' as it is to 'variety', and 'variety' to 'glory' and 'story', and so on. One could ether read this stanza as breaking almost all the rules of rhyme, or as a tour de force in rhyme even where the rules do not require it. The stanza is free by using its trivial artificiality. The narrator's redundant offer of an alternative in the last line 'ride or walk', a technique often used in *Beppo* too, also lifts the trivia of conversational manner into the surprising context of verse.

The politics of these devices are made explicit in the second stanza quoted above – 'there's no servility/In mine irregularity of chime'. Manfred at the end of his play, and our narrator in *Don Juan*, are free, but they have to use their lives, their verse, in order for their freedom to mean. When the narrator writes, two stanzas later, 'I was born for opposition', he does not mean the absolute opposition of a Prometheus – indeed, as he points out in the next stanza, if the people become the rulers, he'll probably have to oppose the people. Opposition does not give identity; on the contrary it gives flexibility, 'mobility' – 'irregularity of chime'. It is this 'infinite variety' which has to be fashioned. In the last canto, the narrator indeed fancies that for one outward identity he has 'two or three within' – probably intentionally going beyond the Faustian dualism of 'two souls' within 'one breast'. As Byron had written in his Journal in 1814, in order to remain true, he had to contradict himself 'on every page'.

Poetry, like emotion in stanzas 1 and 2 of the canto, rounds 'off an hour upon a time'. It staves off the nothingness of 'ennui'. Along with the political imperative of an act of freedom, poetry almost carries with it the moral imperative of an action against *accidie*. The couplet of this stanza is typical of many in the poem. It introduces a fanciful (often weak, often polysyllabic) rhyme, which both makes the reader aware of the intractability of the medium – and therefore renders the sense contingent – and also renders the reader aware of the skill of the narrator – and therefore of the fact that meaning can be salvaged from anything. It is like a Houdini escape from the jaws of linguistic disaster.

The narrator describes his poem as a 'conundrum of a dish' in XV.21, and by XV.62 it has turned into a dish in some literal sense, when a description of a meal is undertaken in mock-heroic style (the original is Agamemnon's feast for Achilles in *The Iliad*). The effect of the description, however, is not so much satirical as a celebration of the power of the narrator's inventiveness in rhyme. Triviality is redeemed by humour. The reduction of poetry to gastronomy is redeemed by the free play of the medium.

There was a goodly 'soupe à la *bonne femme*,'
Though God knows whence it came from; there was too
A turbot for relief of those who cram,
Relieved with dindon à la Périgueux;
There also was – the sinner that I am!
How shall I get this gourmand stanza through? –
Soupe à la Beauveau, whose relief was Dory,
Relieved itself by pork, for greater glory.

. . . .

Fowls à la Condé, slices eke of salmon,
With sauces Genevoises, and haunch of venison;
Wines too which might have slain young Ammon –
A man like whom I hope we shan't see many soon;
They also set a glazed Westphalian ham on,
Whereon Apicius would bestow his benison;
And then there was Champagne with foaming whirls,
As white as Cleopatra's melted pearls.

(*DJ*XV.63, 65)

The coup de grace of course is once again the terminal through-rhyme in the second stanza quoted ('–on' in both 'a' and 'b' rhymes). Not to mention the use of two words to carry the penultimate rhyme of both rhymes: vension/many soon/benison, and salmon/Ammon/ham on. A highly elaborate and ceremonial meal is celebrated, comically, in highly elaborate and sophisticated verse. Art is partly artifice, and partly creation. It draws attention to our dependence on artifice, and yet makes sense of the trivial.

If one is to attempt to sum up the experience of *Don Juan*, one could probably do little better than turn to the first three lines of the penultimate stanza of the poem as we have it:

I leave the thing a problem, like all things: –
The morning came – and breakfast, tea and toast,
Of which most men partake, but no one sings.

(*DJ*XVII.13.1–3)

But *Don Juan* does sing the human, both the problems and the toast.

THE VISION OF JUDGMENT

Given its title, it might be assumed that *The Vision of Judgment* does not sing the human. On the contrary. Whereas Robert Southey's poem *A Vision of Judgement* purports to celebrate ('canonize' in Byron's words) George III by describing his entry into heaven and attacking his liberal opponents, Byron mocks the pretensions of those who judge. Whether the judgement is human or divine barely matters for Byron's poem, which though set at the gates of heaven is roundly humanistic in tone. Byron in his Preface goes through the motions of defending himself from blasphemy, but his key point is about toleration:

> With regard to the supernatural personages treated of, I can only say that I know as much about them, and (as an honest man) have a better right to talk of them than Robert Southey. I have also treated them more tolerantly. The way in which that poor insane creature, the Laureate, deals about his judgments in the next world, is like his own judgment in this. If it was not completely ludicrous, it would be something worse. (McGann, *Lord Byron: Complete Poetical Works*, vol. vi, pp. 310–11)

Byron had been particularly annoyed by Southey's attack (in the Preface to his *Vision*) which referred to him as the leader of the 'Satanic School' of poetry. And at the core of that annoyance was his sense that Southey was a traitor and a hypocrite. Southey had been fanatical on two sides of the fence, the liberal and the conservative extremes. It is the fanaticism, not the point of view, which is morally culpable. Byron's *Vision* is a mixture of personal and political vituperation, but its basic texture is the same as that of *Don Juan*. Only the individual can judge himself. It is absurd, but also dangerous, to believe that one has privileged access to a truth which can be applied to others. And so in Byron's poem George, though no hero, is also no villain – his private life is some recompense for his public failings.

The poem presents the 'legal' dispute between Satan and Michael over the fate of George. Satan and Michael have a kind of humane professional regard for each other:

> Yet still between his Darkness and his Brightness
> There passed a mutual glance of great politeness.

> . . . .
> Then he address'd himself to Satan: 'Why –
> My good old friend, for such I deem you, though
> Our different parties make us fight so shy,
> I ne'er mistake you for a *personal* foe;
> Our difference is *political*, and I
> Trust that, whatever may occur below,
> You know my great respect for you; and this
> Makes me regret whate'er you do amiss...
>
> (*VJ*35.7–8; st.62)

This practical approach is set against the fanatical 'Bob Southey raving'. Witnesses are called – the liberal and piratical Wilkes, who refuses to condemn George utterly; Junius, the anonymous political commentator, whose testimony, while extreme, is made vacuous by its author's anonymity; and Southey himself, who having just died defends himself by attempting to read his *Vision* as the definitive judgement on George:

> But talking about trumpets, here's my Vision!
> Now you shall judge, all people; yes, you shall
> Judge with my judgment! and by my decision
> Be guided who shall enter heaven or fall!
> I settle all these things by intuition,
> Times present, past, to come, heaven, hell and all...
>
> (*VJ*101.1–6)

But by the third line the entire assembled host can bear no more, and chaos ensues as everyone tries to escape. By the fifth line, Peter knocks Southey down, but instead of falling into hell he ends up in one of the Lake District lakes (Southey, with Wordsworth and Coleridge, spent enough time in the Lake District to be thought of as a 'Lake poet'), where:

> He first sunk to the bottom – like his works,
> But soon rose to the surface – like himself...
> (*VJ*105.1–2)

Not even Southey is damned – yet. As for George:

> All I saw farther in the last confusion,
> Was, that King George slipp'd into heaven for one;
> And when the tumult dwindled to a calm,
> I left him practising the hundredth psalm.
>
> (*VJ*106.5–8)

71

The poem in the end refuses to judge – George is in heaven, but by happy accident, as it were. The faint absurdity of George 'practising' the hundredth psalm suggests an almost domestic scene, and a continuity of life beyond the poem, which has little or nothing to do with Heaven and Hell, and a great deal to do, once again, with toleration. It is almost as if, with the narrator, we wave George goodbye. Politics and systematically held convictions are unreliable, at best. Wilkes's, even more Southey's, can invert, while Junius's are all air. Michael and Satan behave decently to each other despite their political roles. In this case it is the angels who are the truly human.

9

Political Action: Italy and Greece

Byron's political stance has in the last twenty years been the subject of some controversy. There are those who would appropriate him to a 'pure' radical position, and revisionists who see him as much more attached to checks and balances, a liberal in the eighteenth-century tradition.

In England his actions were essentially those of the Whig party; his talk from time to time sounded as if it came from the radical extreme. Once in exile, but thinking of the English situation, he again from time to time sounded a positively revolutionary note, but that is always tempting from a distance. When his friend Hobhouse was actually imprisoned for his politics, Byron almost violently upbraided him for getting mixed up with the actions of 'the mob'. There is not much in his considered writing that suggests he was in any sense a modern democrat. On the other hand, the exercise of arbitrary power, whether political or economic, he clearly found obscene.

However, his involvement in politics in Italy and in Greece is easier to evaluate. In both places there was a preliminary task to be done, the morality of which was simple – the removal of an occupying power. Only when he became involved in the succeeding question – 'then what?' – did he once again find it difficult to commit himself to one route rather than another, and become tired of the necessary manoeuvring. His commitment to what we would now call self-determination at a national level is unambiguous. But this commitment does not transcend the practical and transform itself into a Utopian faith – Byron was well aware that a nation's freedom was a 'preliminary' basis only. He had no faith that freedom would produce a just society by itself. Indeed he was highly sceptical of the Greeks' ability to participate in the founding of a society without corruption. In the Greek war of independence, he almost fought in spite of his lack of faith in the participants' morality.

In Italy his connection with the Gamba family, Teresa's relations, drew him directly into clandestine revolutionary activity. He joined a group of the Carboneria (the freedom fighters) known as La Turba – the Mob. The name reflected a majority of working-class members, and it is difficult to think of Byron being happy with this association in England (almost exactly that for which he had castigated Hobhouse). But not only were the Gambas members, it was a group more given to action and less to the abstract talk which characterized (Byron felt) too much of the movement. Following an uprising in Naples in 1820, there was for a while a serious possibility of violent insurrection in Ravenna, in which Byron would certainly have played a significant role. His practical involvement indeed extended to the supply and storage of arms, and also to using his connections to access government mail. Nevertheless a cause never came before a person, and when the local commandant of the government troops was shot outside his house, he risked his position with the Carbonari by taking the dying man into his house and doing everything possible to make him comfortable. He risked considerably more on the other side by sending a letter offering financial support to the Neapolitan revolution-aries, via a courier who was captured, but who succeeded (apparently) in swallowing the documents he was carrying. Eventually the Gambas were arrested and exiled – possibly being exiled rather than imprisoned as a device to get Byron to follow them out of Ravenna, which eventually he did, the group reconstituting itself at Pisa. The Gambas however had to keep on the move, first trying for asylum in Lucca, and then in Genoa. Meanwhile Byron's own presence in Pisa was as comforting to the government there as it had been in Ravenna, a fact not at all helped by a street brawl which left a soldier seriously wounded by one of Byron's servants.

Shelley had joined him in Pisa (indeed had awaited his arrival). For a while the friends replayed their conversations of Switzerland and Venice. As well as his work on *Don Juan* Byron was hard at work on a series of dramatic poems, meditations in some sense on the nature of power in society. He was also theorizing on the nature of literary aesthetics. But on 8 July Shelley, sailing back to his own house from a visit to Byron near Leghorn, where the latter had rented a summer house, was caught in a storm, his boat overwhelmed, and he and his companions drowned. Byron was deeply moved by his death, and felt guilty that he had not made even more of Shelley than he had. He and his companions, the adventurer Trelawny and the radical writer Leigh Hunt who at Shelley's insistence he was supporting, cremated Shelley's remains on the beach. Byron swam out to sea in the direction from which the body had been washed ashore.

The Gambas were eventually forced to move on to Genoa, and Byron felt morally obliged to follow them, though he toyed with setting off for America. He too had in any case to leave Pisa.

His health began to decline. He had the experience of Shelley's death close to him. The Italian cause was stalled. And then, at Hobhouse's urging in London, a member of the London Greek Committee visited him, to urge him to support the cause of Greek independence, and if possible to come to Greece himself. His last days in Italy were soured by a row with Hunt and Mary Shelley over money, which left all sides embittered (despite Byron's previous considerable generosity to both, or possibly because of it). On 21 July 1823, in the company of Trelawny and Teresa's brother Pietro, Byron, having arranged his finances to support the expedition, set sail on what was to prove the last leg of his own pilgrimage.

Byron and his group landed at Cephalonia, an island off the west coast of Greece, where they befriended the English Governor (an odd irony in this fight for independence), who despite maintaining a façade of neutrality was a supporter of Greek independence. They remained on Cephalonia while attempting to understand and evaluate the factional strife that was endemic to the freedom fighters on the mainland. George Finlay, the Greek historian who was on the island at the time, noted Byron's realistic assessment of the Greeks, comparing it favourably to the military enthusiasm of the Governor, himself nobody's fool. As 1823 was drawing to a close Byron was eventually persuaded to join the Greek Mavrocordatos at Missolonghi, opposite Patras, where he had first landed so many years before. His voyage there was an exciting one, for his boat almost ran into a Turkish man-of-war in the night, and escaped only by dodging from cove to cove northwards along the coast, before eventually being rescued by a Greek escort, and sailing back south to Missolonghi on 4 January 1824. Meantime Pietro Gamba, travelling in another boat laden with guns and money, was captured by a Turkish vessel, and was only allowed to leave Patras with his ship through a coincidence worthy of *Don Juan* – the captain of his ship having saved the life of the Turkish captain in a shipwreck years before!

Byron and Gamba were joining the representative of the Greek committee, Colonel Stanhope, in what was a dismal marshy town. As well as paying for troops, Byron supported a field hospital and, somewhat sceptically, a propaganda publication. The first months of 1824 were taken up by planning a military expedition to Lepanto, which never happened, and by orchestrating the arrival through the Turkish blockade of further resources from England. Finally in March there was talk of a summit meeting of the Greek factional leaders at Salona, but bad weather prevented even that journey, and the Turks reinforced their coastal blockade.

Since his arrival, Byron had been de facto the 'ruler' not only of the mixed bag of assembled military, but of the town as well. Disputes, calls for money, the disentangling of corruption were the routine of his days. He had suffered severe attacks of illness in March (with some symptoms which suggest a neurological problem), and in the middle of April he fell ill again, apparently with a fever. On the 19th, he died. The cause of his death has been much disputed, and is perhaps of little interest, except to the medical detective. Stroke, kidney failure, fever aggravated by incompetent medical treatment, have all been canvassed. There is a poetic sense in which he had reached an end in life, and paradoxically progress, both to his poetic reputation, and even more to his hopes for Greek independence, could best be achieved by his death.

He was to become a hero, in both England and Greece, almost as instantly after his death as he had suddenly become famous in life.

10

The Late Dramas

From *Manfred* on, Byron wrote a series of works in dramatic form, though he often insisted that they were not intended for production. He claimed at some length (for example in the Prefaces to *Marino Faliero* and *Sardanapalus*) that these dramas were modelled on Aristotle's principles, observing the unities of time, action and place, and eschewing the Shakespearean tradition of the English stage. This was part of his general attack on Romantic self-indulgence, and his stout defence of the poetry of Pope and the eighteenth century. It should be noted though that the underlying rationale of this defence is not very eighteenth-century-like. It depends on the premise that the individual is the ultimate meaning-giver in life, and therefore needs the support of civilized (but artificial – in the linguist's sense 'conventional') decorum in order not to fall into solipsistic chaos. The earlier period started from the opposite presumption – that civilized decorum was an absolute mirror of universal truth and the very opposite of human hubris. Byron's insistence on 'art' over 'nature' is closer to the twentieth century than it is to the eighteenth.

The only one of these plays to have substantial repeated success on stage was *Werner*, which became something of a box-office hit in the nineteenth century, in an acting version edited by the actor and impresario William Macready. But most of the plays had a significant cultural impact, even if not on the stage. *Manfred*, most obviously, as well as entering into the canon of literary texts and the history of ideas, produced orchestral works by Schumann and Tchaikovsky. *Sardanapalus* is the subject of a painting by Delacroix, as is *Marino Faliero*. *Cain* became a *cause célèbre* over its supposed blasphemy, and is revived from time to time in small-scale productions to the present day. All of this is in stark contrast to the dramas of Byron's poetic contemporaries – Coleridge's for example – whose theatre works have sunk far deeper than Southey in his lake. But this may have more to do with Byron's fame, than with the intrinsic merits of the plays. However, though they never rise to the level of *Don Juan*, *Werner* and *Cain* in particular do have some metrical interest, and most share with their progenitor, *Manfred*, a clear thematic structure, almost like a laboratory experiment, which can reveal a lot about Byron's thinking. In these later plays, the metaphysics of *Manfred* resolved, this thinking is mainly political, even in a 'biblical' drama such as *Cain*. *Marino Faliero*, *Sardanapalus*, *The Two Foscari*, *Cain*, *Heaven and Earth*, *Werner*, and the fragmentary *Deformed Transformed* were all written in a very short space of time between 1820 and 1822, when, as we have seen, Byron was deeply involved in Italian politics. We shall sample *Faliero*, *Foscari*, *Cain*, and *Werner*.

Faliero and *Foscari* are both set in Venice, and both revolve around the structure of power in a republic. The question is to what extent, in a structure which is 'democratic' (not in the modern sense of the term but relative to a monarchy held by 'divine right'), does the individual's right to personal dignity supersede duty to the state. In other words, this reframes in political terms the consequences of the philosophical position reached by the end of *Manfred*. If there is no absolute standard of duty, how should one negotiate personal and social responsibility, the former being the only true responsibility, but the latter being a necessary artifice for the continuation of both society and, paradoxically, meaningful personal existence.

Structurally, the two plays are indeed very similar. In the case of *Faliero*, a presumed personal insult, which goes effectively unpunished by the state, is part of the motivating force which leads the elected head of state, the Doge Faliero, to plot against it. In *Foscari*, the Doge Foscari is caught between his duty to protect the state and his familial ties, when his only surviving son is accused of treachery. In both plays it is clear that the state apparatus is being manipulated by others, every bit as much as it may be under threat from its head. The state is the only bulwark against selfish anarchy, and yet the state is itself constituted by people constantly torn between civic and personal values (and in the cases of both Foscari and Faliero themselves these personal values may seem to be the most justified).

The irresolvability of these issues leads to tragedy in both cases, but not primarily to the personal tragedy of the two compromised 'heroes', rather to tragedy for the state. These are not plays advocating revolution, nor self-sanctioned action, even where they are deeply critical of corrupt institutions. The removal of absolute control makes negotiated control vitally necessary, but that control seems inevitably compromised, or perhaps corrupted, by personal interest. In both plays domestic love, represented by women, Angiolina in *Faliero* and Marina in *Foscari*, is a conceivable alternative to a civic power structure, but is not allowed to carry sufficient force to emerge as a realistic possibility.

In *Cain*, the love of Adah for Cain does emerge as a possible solution to Cain's troubles, but it is a solution which Cain ignores. Here the metaphysical and political are profoundly interwoven. It is Cain's obsession with the value of individual life which leads him to take it, and his refusal of authority in the name of freedom which leads him into an act which deprives his brother of all freedom. Cain is taken by Lucifer on a voyage into space where he learns not the secrets of the Universe, but rather his own minuscule place within it. The search for meaning only produces a sense of worthlessness. Lucifer's advice bears a striking resemblance to the Prometheus poem, and even to *Manfred*:

> *One good* gift has the fatal apple given –
> Your *reason*: – let it not be over-sway'd
> By tyrannous threats to force you into faith
> 'Gainst all external sense and inward feeling:
> Think and endure, – and form an inner world
> In your own bosom – where the outward fails;
> So shall you nearer be the spiritual
> Nature, and war triumphant with your own.
>
> (*Cain*, II.ii.459–66)

Cain of course does not take this advice – he loses his faculty of reason at the key moment, and blindly lunges at Abel as the (guiltless) representative of his 'oppressor'. But Lucifer is himself manipulating a power structure – he wants to force Cain into the 'Promethean' position of absolute opposition, where his identity *is* that opposition, rather than Manfred's position of freedom even from opposition. Cain's self-absorption leads to the opposite of freedom – an obsession with oppression. Cain's fractured isolation is dramatically rendered by Byron's use of the metrical line. Here is an extract including Cain's first speech:

> *Adah* God, the Eternal! Parent of all things!
> Who didst create these best and beauteous beings,
> To be beloved, more than all, save thee –
> Let me love thee and them: – All hail! all hail!
> *Zillah* Oh, God! who loving, making, blessing all,
> Yet didst permit the serpent to creep in,
> And drive my father forth from Paradise,
> Keep us from further evil: – Hail! all hail!
> *Adam* Son Cain, my first-born, wherefore art thou silent?
> *Cain* Why should I speak?
> *Adam*   To pray.
> *Cain*   Have ye not pray'd?
> *Adam* We have, most fervently.
> *Cain*   And loudly: I
> Have heard you.

(Cain, I.i.14–25)

Cain cannot 'complete' either himself or a pentameter line – whereas the family group speak in closed symmetry. Though the character of Cain has sympathetic energy (and Adam passively and Eve shrewishly are not sympathetically portrayed) it is difficult to emerge from the play blaming anyone other than Cain for the tragedy. This is reinforced by the pounding self-obsession of the closing line (or rather, since it is Cain speaking, part line):

> *Adah* Peace be with him! [Abel]
> *Cain*   But with *me*!' –

(Cain, III.i.561)

If Cain's character returns us to the politics of opposition, his play does not. If anything has been learned, it emerges only in Cain's plea to Adah:

> No more of threats: we have had too many of them:
> Go to our children; I will follow thee.

(Cain, III.i.525–6)

The 'threats' may hint at the interdiction on the fruit as well as Cain's own and Adah's here, but somewhere there may be hope in the domestic bond. Cain's closing words however make even this doubtful. This is an uncomfortable play, but it scarcely warrants Southey's 'Satanic' label, and it is no incitement to armed revolution.

Of all the dramas, *Werner* is the most clear-cut in its

condemnation of the cult of the self. Ulric, Werner's son, represents the nadir of the politics of unrestrained Romantic opposition. Without civilized restraint, the handing over of responsibility from absolute authority to the individual will end in disaster. The plot can be rendered simply – though in the execution it is not. The time is the Thirty Years' War. Werner, in exile, banished by his own father for unruly behaviour, wants to kill Stralenheim, a nobleman who is pursuing him. His son Ulric guesses this and kills Stralenheim himself, without at this point admitting the fact to his father. Upon his father's death, the once unruly Werner gratefully takes over his family title. Ulric reveals, to Werner's horror, that not only did he kill Stralenheim, but that he leads a band of outlaw soldiers exploiting the anarchy of the war. Werner realizes that his family has lost its title to power forever. The son's half-hearted rebellion against his father is carried to its logical anarchic conclusion – the grandson behaves in the way the father 'wanted' to behave. The women, Werner's wife Josephine and Ulric's betrothed Ida (the daughter of Stralenheim), who represent again a domestic middle-way between feudal order and rank individualism, are the casualties of the men's obsessions. As in *Cain*, the verse given to Ulric is notably fractured, while that given to Josephine is the smoothest (and is steeped too in imagery of nature).

Werner does not strictly follow the 'unities' Byron champions, but in the tightness of its thematic structure it follows them in spirit, while allowing itself Shakespearean changes of mood and place. *Faliero* and *Foscari* are both claustrophobic, and, if we allow for the space journey, so too is *Cain*. This depressing claustrophobic feel extends to all the dramas. None of them proposes a political solution to the loosening structure of society – a loosening of which Byron of course politically approves, despite its potential for disaster. They represent the negative to *Don Juan's* positive. Their adoption of the classical unities mirrors *Juan's* adoption of ottava rima – both regulatory forms making sense out of potential chaos. But the 'syllogisms' of the dramas lead only to a clearer understanding of where failure lies in wait. They bear a very close relationship to Byron's personal experience of political action in the last years of his life, which seemed to lead inevitably nowhere.

The joy of the ottava rima is the creation of a space where freedom can find a social place and yet remain itself. This is Byron's real gift to the world.

Select Bibliography

WORKS BY BYRON

Marchand, Leslie A. (ed.), *Byron's Letters and Journals* (London: John Murray, 1973–94).

McGann, Jerome J. (ed.), *Lord Byron: The Complete Poetical Works* (Oxford: Clarendon Press, 1980–93).

Nicholson, Andrew (ed.), *Lord Byron: The Complete Miscellaneous Prose* (Oxford: Clarendon Press, 1991).

Reiman, Donald H. (ed.), *The Manuscripts of the Younger Romantics* (New York and London: Garland, 1985–). Has interesting editions (by J. J. McGann, Peter Cochran, Andrew Nicholson, and others) of many of Byron's poems showing clearly his manuscript working methods.

BIOGRAPHY

Crompton, Louis, *Byron and Greek Love* (London: Faber, 1985). Interesting, though one-track, exploration of Byron's 'homosexuality' and its context.

Eisler, Benita, *Byron: Child of Passion, Full of Fame* (London: Hamish Hamilton, 1999). A controversial new biography which does not add much substantively to Marchand, and has a marked viewpoint, but is written in an accessible style.

Marchand, Leslie A., *Byron: A Biography* (New York: Alfred A. Knopf, 1957). The standard biography and a model of good scholarship.

CRITICISM

Barton, Anne, *Byron: Don Juan*, Landmarks in World Literature Series (Cambridge: Cambridge University Press, 1992). A very good introduction to the poem.

Beatty, Bernard, *Byron's Don Juan* (Totowa, NJ: Barnes & Noble, 1985). An interesting but sophisticated reading of the poem, combining the religious with what might be called the postmodernist.

Beatty, Bernard and Newey, Vincent (eds), *Byron and the Limits of Fiction* (Liverpool: Liverpool University Press, 1988). A very good collection of essays – almost but not all of a post-structuralist slant.

Beaty, Frederick L., *Byron the Satirist* (De Kalb: Northern Illinois University Press, 1985).

Cooke, Michael G., *The Blind Man Traces the Circle: On the Patterns and Philosophy of Byron's Poetry* (Princeton, NJ: Princeton University Press, 1969). One of the first 'modern' studies of Byron.

Elfenbein, Andrew, *Byron and the Victorians* (Cambridge: Cambridge University Press, 1995). Particularly interesting on gender questions.

Franklin, Caroline, *Byron's Heroines* (Oxford: Clarendon Press, 1992).

Galperin, William H., *The Return of the Visible in British Romanticism* (Baltimore, MD: Johns Hopkins Press, 1993). A psychoanalytically informed reading of Byron amongst much else.

Garber, Frederick, *Self, Text, and Romantic Irony: The Example of Byron* (Princeton, NJ: Princeton University Press, 1988). A balanced account of the relationship between Byron's irony and its more extreme forms.

Graham, Peter W., *Don Juan and Regency England* (Charlottesville and London: University of Virginia Press, 1990).

Haslett, Moyra, *Byron's Don Juan and the Don Juan Legend* (Oxford: Clarendon Press, 1997). Not always reliable, but provides useful contextual information.

Hoagwood, Terence Allan, *Byron's Dialectic: Skepticism and the Critique of Culture* (Lewisburg, NJ: Bucknell University Press, 1993). A postmodernist reading. Useful on the prose writings which conditioned Byron's writing.

Keach, William, 'Political Inflection in Byron's *Ottava Rima*', *Studies in Romanticism*, 27 (1988), 551–62. An interesting close-reading.

Kelsall, Malcolm, *Byron's Politics* (Brighton: Harvester, 1987). The soundest book on Byron's politics – but does not please those who see him as an out-and-out revolutionary.

Lansdown, Richard, *Byron's Historical Dramas* (Oxford: Clarendon Press, 1992).

Leask, Nigel, *British Romantic Writers and the East: Anxieties of Empire* (Cambridge: Cambridge University Press, 1992).

McGann, Jerome J., 'The Book of Byron and the Book of a World', *The Beauty of Inflections: Literary Investigations in Historical Method and Theory* (Oxford: Clarendon Press, 1985). A short way into McGann's later thinking on Byron.

———— *Don Juan in Context* (Chicago: Chicago University Press, 1979).

83

Manning, Peter J., *Byron and His Fictions* (Detroit: Wayne State University Press, 1978). One of the earliest psychoanalytic readings.

Richardson, Alan, *A Mental Theatre: Poetic Drama and Consciousness in the Romantic Age* (University Park and London: Pennsylvania State University Press, 1988).

Martin, Philip W., *Byron: A Poet Before His Public* (Cambridge: Cambridge University Press, 1982). Byron and his audience.

Rutherford, Andrew, *Byron: A Critical Heritage* (London: Routledge & Kegan Paul, 1970).

Shilstone, Frederick W., *Approaches to Teaching Byron's Poetry* (New York: MLA, 1991).

Stabler, Jane (ed.), *Byron*, Longman Critical Readers (London and New York: Longman, 1998). The best collection of modern critical essays.

Vassallo, Peter, *Byron: The Italian Literary Influence* (New York: St Martin's Press, 1984).

Wolfson, Susan J., *Formal Charges: The Shaping of Poetry in British Romanticism* (Stanford, CA: Stanford University Press, 1997).

Wood, Nigel (ed.), *Don Juan*, Theory in Practice Series (Buckingham: Open University Press, 1993).

USEFUL JOURNALS

Byron Journal
Keats–Shelley Journal
Keats–Shelley Review
Romanticism

Index